Social exclusion

DAVID BYRNE

OPEN UNIVERSITY PRESS
Buckingham • Philadelphia

Open University Press
Celtic Court
22 Ballmoor
Buckingham
MK18 1XW

e-mail: enquiries@openup.co.uk
world wide web: http://www.openup.co.uk

and
325 Chestnut Street
Philadelphia, PA 19106, USA

First Published 1999

A catalogue record of this book is available from the British Library

ISBN   0 335 19974 7 (pbk)   0 335 19975 5 (hbk)

Library of Congress Cataloging-in-Publication Data
Byrne, D.S. (David S.), 1947–
    Social exclusion / David Byrne.
       p.   cm. — (Issues in society)
    Includes bibliographical references.
    ISBN 0–335–19975–5   ISBN 0–335–19974–7 (pbk)
    1. Marginality, Social.   2. Marginality, Social—Philosophy.
 3. Poor.   4. Equality.   5. Social policy.   I. Title.   II. Series.
 HM136.B97   1999
 305—dc21   98–55527
                                                                CIP

Typeset by Graphicraft Limited, Hong Kong
Printed in Great Britain by St Edmundsbury Press, Bury St Edmunds, Suffolk

Social exclusion

ISSUES IN SOCIETY
Series Editor: Tim May

Current and forthcoming titles

This book is dedicated to Clare, Alissa and Sally

Contents

Series editor's foreword

The social sciences contribute to a greater understanding of the dynamics of social life and explanations for the workings of societies in general. They are often not given due credit for this role and much writing has been devoted to why this should be the case. At the same time, we are living in an age in which the role of science in society is being re-evaluated. This has led to both a defence of science as the disinterested pursuit of knowledge and an attack on science as nothing more than an institutionalized assertion of faith with no greater claim to validity than mythology and folklore. These debates tend to generate more heat than light.

In the meantime, the social sciences, in order to remain vibrant and relevant, will reflect the changing nature of these public debates. In so doing, they provide mirrors upon which we can gaze in order to understand not only what we have been and what we are now, but to inform ideas about what we might become. This is not simply about understanding the reasons people give for their actions in terms of the contexts in which they act, as well as analysing the relations of cause and effect in the social, political and economic spheres, but also concerns the hopes, wishes and aspirations that people, in their different cultural ways, hold.

In any society that claims to have democratic aspirations, these hopes and wishes are not for the social scientist to prescribe. For this to happen it would mean that the social sciences were able to predict human behaviour with certainty. This would require one theory and one method applicable to all times and places. The physical sciences do not live up to such stringent criteria, whilst the conditions in societies which provided for this outcome, were it even possible, would be intolerable. Why? Because a necessary condition of human freedom is the ability to have acted otherwise and thus to imagine and practice different ways of organizing societies and living together.

It does not follow from the above that social scientists do not have a valued role to play, as is often assumed in ideological attacks upon their place and function within society. After all, in focusing upon what we have been and what we are now, what we might become is inevitably illuminated. Therefore, while it may not be the province of the social scientist to predict our futures, they are, given not only their understandings and explanations, but equal positions as citizens, entitled to engage in public debates concerning future prospects.

This new international series was devised with this general ethos in mind. It seeks to offer students of the social sciences, at all levels, a forum in which ideas and topics of interest are interrogated in terms of their importance for understanding key social issues. This is achieved through a connection between style, structure and content that aims to be both illuminating and challenging in terms of its evaluation of those issues, as well as representing an original contribution to the subject under discussion.

Given this underlying philosophy, this series will contain books on topics which are driven by substantive interests. This is not simply a reactive endeavour in terms of reflecting dominant social and political preoccupations, it is also proactive in terms of an examination of issues which relate to and inform the dynamics of social life and the structures of society that are often not part of public discourse. Thus, what is distinctive about this series is an interrogation of the assumed characteristics of our current epoch in relation to its consequences for the organization of society and social life, as well as its appropriate mode of study.

Each contribution will contain, for the purposes of general orientation, as opposed to rigid structure, three parts. First, an interrogation of the topic which is conducted in a manner that renders explicit core assumptions surrounding the issues and/or an examination of the consequences of historical trends for contemporary social practices. Second, a section which aims to 'bring alive' ideas and practices by considering the ways in which they directly inform the dynamics of social relations. A third section will then move on to make an original contribution to the topic. This will encompass possible future forms and content, likely directions for the study of the phenomena in question, or an original analysis of the topic itself. Of course, it might be a combination of all three.

David Byrne's book is written with this ethos in mind. When it is asserted that we are living through a political epoch defined by a 'third way', this encapsulates not only an assertion of difference from past programmes of social reform, but is also seen to represent a vision of an alternative mode of organizing society and social relations that does not replicate mistakes of the past. To this extent it might be reasonable to assert that a balance is needed that does not appear to take the thesis of an 'end of history' for granted: that is, capitalism is vindicated and the administration of 'inclusion' is the topic for consideration, as opposed to an explanation of the dynamics of exclusion based upon the systems under and through which people operate in their daily lives.

To offer a critique of the consequences of a system which is so much taken-for-granted is bound to be controversial. At the same time, within academic discussions it is modernity and postmodernity that seem to pre-occupy authors, whilst mention of the dynamics and effects of capitalism as an economic system is not so prevalent. Therefore, by default, it is as if we must live with an economic system that the process of historical evolution has vindicated as being its final resting place. To even imagine alternatives via a critique of present conditions thereby becomes a daunting task in the face of such overwhelming complacency and indifference to the plight of the excluded.

Robust and spirited in its style and methodical and comparative in its content, no reader will emerge from this book believing that the author prevaricates when it comes to the dynamics and consequences of social exclusion. Arguing that post-industrial capitalism and its related social politics is converging around a norm of structural social exclusion and labour market flexibility, he argues that this is driven by ideology and the subordination of social policies to an anticipation of business interests, *as if* such interests were simply separate from the process of social reproduction.

This 'phase shift' in the social order through which we are living in the West, encapsulated by the term post-industrial capitalism, is not an inevitable process, but the outcome of interactions between decisions that inform the construction of social policies and the economic order. Drawing upon complexity theory, David Byrne argues that whilst social exclusion is an inherent feature of contemporary capitalism and that chaotic processes are deterministic, agency can nevertheless make a difference. To that extent, actions, either at the level of the single household or the collective, can change circumstances; the question is with what overall effects?

Seeking comparative explanations for social exclusion according to the tenets of complexity theory raises serious issues for the construction of social policies. In particular, it does not relieve individual nation-states of the burden of responsibility for ameliorating and responding to the consequences of an unbridled capitalism in the age of globalization. It also directly challenges the idea that the solution to the problem of social exclusion comes with changing individual skills in order to make people more marketable according to the demands of market capitalism. From that point of view, this book is controversial in directly challenging contemporary trends. Yet in an age where the complacency of some is bought at the cost of the misery of others with its effects on the fabric of social order for all, the arguments in this book deserve serious consideration and debate.

Tim May

Acknowledgements

I would like to acknowledge the domestic support and attention of Alissa, Clare and Sally Ruane to whom this book is dedicated. Those who helped me with ideas and discussion include Sally Ruane, Tim Blackman and John Ditch (as by-products of their help in a Teaching Quality Assessment process), Gill Callaghan, Liz Wilkie and Tim Rogers. My students have acted both as a sounding board and as a source of information about how the world is really working. Finally, I would like to acknowledge the considerable encouragement and support of Tim May, the editor of this series.

Introduction

> *Exclusion* is an idea which poses the right kind of questions.
> (Donnison 1998: 5, original emphasis)

The expression 'social exclusion' is now widely employed in debates about the social politics of Europe. It is a new phrase in English language argument, although it has a longer European history, particularly in France. To a considerable, and welcome, extent, it has replaced that pejorative US import, 'the underclass', in discussions about the poor in 'post-industrial' society. There are advantages in this development. The two words 'social' and 'exclusion' when put together conjoin society as a whole, as opposed to the discrete individuals within society, with ongoing process, as opposed to timeless state. When we talk and write about 'social exclusion' we are talking about changes in the whole of society which have consequences for some of the people in that society. We are dealing, as C. Wright Mills (1959) suggested we always ought to in sociology, with the intersection of history and biography – with the way the social world changes and with the consequences of those changes for the lives that people lead.

Note that the term 'social exclusion' is inherently dynamic: exclusion happens in time, in a time of history, and 'determines' the lives of the individuals and collectivities who are excluded *and* of those individuals and collectivities who are not.[1] Note also that although the term is clearly systemic, that is to say it is about the character of the social system and about the dynamic development of social structures, at the same time it has implications for agency. 'Exclusion' is something that is done by some people to other people. The central tenet of popular versions of 'the underclass' argument is that miserable conditions are self-induced – the poor do it to themselves. Political theorists of social exclusion allow that they can be consequences of economic transformation; it is the fault of 'society' as a whole. So far only dangerous radicals, like the Catholic Bishops of England and Wales, admit that the people who stand to gain might have something to do with it – that they might be shaping the character of economic and social arrangements, the very stuff of social politics, to their own advantage and to the disadvantage of others.

It is important to distinguish the idea of 'social exclusion' from the somewhat simpler notion of 'poverty'. Walker and Walker (1997) do this:

> we have retained the distinction regarding *poverty* as a lack of the material resources, especially income, necessary to participate in British society and *social exclusion* as a more comprehensive formulation which refers to the dynamic process of being shut out, fully or partially, from any of the social, economic, political or cultural systems which determine the social integration of a person in society. Social exclusion may, therefore, be seen as the denial (or non-realisation) of the civil, political and social rights of citizenship.
>
> (A. Walker and C. Walker 1997: 8; original emphases)

Another definition is offered by Madanipour *et al.* (1998):

> Social exclusion is defined as a multi-dimensional process, in which various forms of exclusion are combined: participation in decision making and political processes, access to employment and material resources, and integration into common cultural processes. When combined, they create acute forms of exclusion that find a spatial manifestation in particular neighbourhoods.
>
> (Madanipour *et al.* 1998: 22)

Generally this book will work with an approach which is closer to that of Madanipour *et al.* than to that of Walker and Walker. I want to place very considerable emphasis on both the multidimensionality of exclusion understood in terms of the complex dynamics of life trajectories, and on the significance of spatial separation within the urban areas of advanced industrial societies.

For Walker and Walker (1997) the opposite of exclusion is integration, with integration understood in relation to the idea of citizenship as it was formulated by Marshall (1950). This view represents a considerable development beyond the passive conception of poverty as a state. However, it takes up only one of the two competing projects of modernity, that centring on the notion of individual rights founded on the doctrine of 'possessive individualism' (MacPherson 1962). This is part of the liberal project of individual emancipation, with the individual understood as unique subject and agent. There is another project, the democratic socialist project of collective transformation, in which the collective actor is the universal working class.[2] Theorists of postmodernity, with that term and that category understood in the most general sense, argue that there is no universal collective social actor, even in terms of inherent potential. Instead we must recognize the existence of a multiplicity of differentiated and potentially competing social collectivities founded around identities which may be as much matters of voluntary choice as of structural determination.

The argument presented here will be unashamedly old-fashioned: social politics in post-industrial capitalism are necessarily organized around the disputes which at an ideological level take the form of confrontations among the three positions of classical liberalism with its foundation in possessive individualism, democratic socialism with its foundation in solidarity, and conservatism with its foundation in the pre-modern conception of an appropriate status-based social order. These categories in practice intermingle and cross-fertilize but they are what matter, precisely because they can be associated with absolutely 'real' and very general material interests.[3]

Another important weakness of contemporary versions of the Marshallian citizenship approach is a relative neglect of issues of power. Marshall himself did not ignore power, but he did not get beyond a consideration of the extension of the franchise in representative democracy. The new school of 'citizenship', even when it does engage with anything more than a very passive conception of rights, seldom gets beyond the notion of the active citizen as the fulfiller of reciprocal obligations of general dogooding and busybodying. In contrast, those, like Madinapour *et al.* (1998), who discuss social exclusion with an urban frame of reference, are inevitably confronted by power as it is exercised by competing interests in the processes of urban governance.

We should not forget that government's concerns with social exclusion may be derived in the first instance from their general role as crisis resolvers. Duffy (1997) has made a useful distinction between the fiscal crises which may result from poverty and the order crises which stem from social exclusion and consequent failures of integration. Of course social exclusion will also contribute to fiscal burdens, even if only through the costs of maintaining social mechanisms directed at limiting disorder, the negative feedback element of governance.

'Social exclusion' is not simply a term in social politics. It is also a central concern of social science, identified by the UK Economic and Social Research Council (ESRC 1996) as one of the key 'thematic priorities' which will guide its funding decisions in the run up to the millennium. It is perhaps significant that this theme ranks nine from nine whereas 'Economic Performance and Development' is placed emphatically first. None the less it is there. However, there is a problem. The academic debate on social exclusion provides an excellent illustration of the problems posed by the reification of disciplinary boundaries within the contemporary academy which prompted the Gulbenkian Commission's (1996) injunction to *Open the Social Sciences*. The processes which engender social exclusion and the issues that derive from it are the subject matter of investigation by both a range of academic disciplines, including sociology, geography, economics, history and political science, and by inter- and multidisciplinary fields which have become established as distinctive academic areas: urban studies, health studies, labour studies and education. In the UK in particular, but increasingly on a European scale, they are the subject matter of that strange academic entity 'social policy', perhaps the oldest of the distinctive inter- and multidisciplinary fields with its origins in late nineteenth and early twentieth century liberal collectivism's concern with poverty, and now making claims to stand as a discipline in its own right. There is a cross-discipline and field debate about this topic but it remains at best only partially coherent, primarily because there are fundamental dissonances in the way in which the processes of social change, which can be subsumed under the heading of 'social exclusion', are conceptualized and above all else measured.

There is an urgent requirement for a synthesis which tackles the problem of the focus on the individual as the object of measurement and conceptualization, characteristic of economics, social policy, and much of quantitative sociology's examination of change through time. In the social sciences there is now a clear and absolutely crucial recognition of the dynamic character of social process but there is also a failure to integrate the individual with the social entities through which individuals lead their lives: households, the complex and multi-layered components of social space, and the social order as a whole. The synthesis we need must be able both to bring together concepts and to provide an account of complex and interacting levels in society.

The objective of this book is to attempt such a synthesis – to clear the ground, establish just what we are dealing with, consider what the origins of it are, and review proposals for doing something about it. It will draw on a range of disciplines and fields and it will employ the understanding of social dynamics offered by the application of the conceptual tools of 'chaos/complexity' to the complex nested systems of the social world. These are new and different ideas. They are not intrinsically difficult but careful attention to them as they all presented will be necessary.

I am far from neutral on the politics of these matters but will endeavour to be honest in my presentation of ideas and 'facts' and clear about my own views so that readers can decide to what extent they influence the presentation of argument and account. I reserve the right, following on from an honourable tradition which will be represented here by citation of Hazlitt, to name things for what they are and to be polemical in so doing, although the text will remain primarily in academic mode with polemic confined to some endnotes and to the conclusion. However, I really do feel that the democratic left has been far too shy in showing that it can bite if vexed. Bite I will.

And now a note of caution. John Veit-Wilson (1998) has made a very important distinction between 'weak' and 'strong' versions of the idea of social exclusion. He puts it like this:

> In the 'weak' version of this discourse, the solutions lie in altering these excluded peoples handicapping characteristics and enhancing their integration into dominant society. 'Stronger' forms of this discourse

also emphasise the role of those who are doing the excluding and therefore aim for solutions which reduce the powers of exclusion.

(Veit-Wilson 1998: 45)

He goes on to note that many consider the development of the discourse of social exclusion in France in the 1980s as being 'a discourse deliberately chosen for closure, to exclude other potential discourses in European political debate and to depoliticize poverty *as far as income redistribution was concerned*' (Veit-Wilson 1998: 97, original emphasis). I think that is right, so long as we talk about the weak version of the idea. Certainly the use of 'social exclusion' in the UK in the late 1990s by New Labour seems to be exactly as a method of closure in relation to challenges to inequality as a general social issue. In this book, unless explicitly qualified, the idea of social exclusion will always be used in its strong sense. Social science has been, rightly, accused of adopting a posture of palms up to the rich for the receipt of funding and eyes down to the poor as part of the surveillance necessary for their control. Here the eyes are definitely looking up more than down.

Structure of the book

The remainder of this introductory chapter describes the organization of the book as a whole. First let me state a central tenet underpinning the whole book: there has been a recent categorical change in the character of advanced industrial societies. The word 'categorical' is used to indicate that this is a change of kind, of quality, rather than some matter of incremental continuous development. To use the vocabulary of chaos/complexity, there has been a phase shift. This book uses the ideas of chaos and complexity to explore the dynamic character of our changing social order. The objective here is to extend our understanding of the significance of the dynamic so that we can use it to describe how our sort of society changes. Indeed we can go beyond description. A proper understanding of the complex character of social dynamics offers the possibility of an informed and engaged social science which plays a role in the shaping of the character of the future. Leisering and Walker (1998a) are absolutely right when they identify the dynamic perspective as:

the beginning of an intellectual revolution, one that blends insight from across the social sciences, merges quantitative and qualitative methodologies, combines micro and macro views of society and exploits the power of international comparison.

(Leisering and Walker 1998a: xiv)

My point is that once we go dynamic, we must go non-linear. We are dealing with emergence, bifurcation, complexity and the possibility of willed alternatives. We are in the realms of a science that deals with the possibility of different forms for the future. That matters a great deal.

The core of this book is organized in two parts. Part one seeks to establish the content of the academic and political debate which deals with these issues. This part comprises three chapters. Chapter 1 examines the classical liberal tradition of political economy with its historic identification of the surplus population/residuum recast in contemporary terms as 'the underclass'. It deals with perspectives which are essentially founded around the doctrines of possessive individualism as these were influenced by the social pessimism of Malthus and by classical political economy's assertion of the market as the epitome of rationality. It should be noted that in this chapter I deal with much of the debate on citizenship, precisely because the late twentieth century version of that idea is constructed around an individualistic conception of rights, and with Etzioni's version of communitarianism, which for me remains essentially founded on individual interests expressed in a utilitarian form, rather than on any notion of emergent solidarity. The general discussion of the residuum/underclass will also be considered here, not because those concerned with that debate necessarily identify with the politics of the 'New' or old Right, but because the debate seems to me to revolve around two themes which are part of the Right's repertoire. These are the notion of surplus population after Malthus and the notion of the non-elect which comes from Calvinistic Protestantism.[4] The introduction of the term 'New Right' illustrates the difficulties of actual classification. That expression describes not only those who assert the economic logic of classical liberalism, an inherently anti-conservative doctrine, but also those who do this in association with a reassertion of traditional social, and especially sexual and familial values, as part of a programme of neo-conservatism. Protestantism's concern with individual salvation through faith without works and Calvinism's justification of the expulsion of the non-elect seems to me to be the linking features here.

Chapter 2 examines both the combination of Rousseau-influenced 'republicanism' and Catholic social thought, which underpins the idea of social exclusion with its Durkheimian overtones of organic solidarity, and the 'collectivist' version of liberalism which is found in the ideas and programmes of Keynes, Marshall himself and Beveridge. What these positions have in common at the most fundamental level is that they are prepared to put politics in control of markets, although they all seek to retain the market as the fundamental form of economic organization.

It has to be recognized that there are some real contradictions in these positions. The French Revolution asserted 'Fraternity', which has an exact non-sexist synonym in socialism's subsequent conception of 'Solidarity'. For all the influence of Locke on republican and democratic thought, the popular masses were able to force their discourse of solidarity into the political lexicon. From the point of view of liberal political economy the discourse of solidarity is deeply reactionary. It is a version of romanticism, often informed by a looking back to some imaginary ideal past. In this respect it has a common element with the Catholic hierarchy's inherent conservatism and defence of the old order with its ranked statuses in which people were included by insertion in their proper place.

However, Christian doctrine, as expressed in that dangerous and re-volutionary set of texts known as the New Testament, does not advocate hierarchy. On the contrary it is profoundly egalitarian in its expression of solidarity. Catholicism had to contain within itself by accommodation the radical challenge represented in the Middle Ages by the Franciscan tradition. It failed to contain, but succeeded in suppressing, the later Hussite opposition.[5] Within the social doctrines of Catholicism there is a contradiction, which the Church sought to resolve in practice in the nineteenth century through its condemnation of the consequences of Godless political economy and endorsement of workers' rights and state welfare. None the less, this contradiction remains immanent in Catholicism; witness the difficulties with the worker priests' tradition in various European countries and with the general programme of liberation theology on a global scale.

The common element in the approaches discussed in Chapter 2 is that while they are solidaristic in objective, they do not assert the necessity for a transformation of capitalism into something else. They are efforts to accommodate an element of solidarity and its inevitable tendency towards equality, with the continued existence of a market economy and its inevitable tendency towards inequality. For this reason I include in the discussions in this chapter a consideration of the set of approaches most usually known by the name of the founder of the tendency, Keynes. Keynesianism is the most important coherent system derived from the collectivist shift taken by much of the UK's liberal intelligentsia in the later nineteenth and early twentieth centuries in response to the intellectual stimulus of the English Hegelians and to the political reality of the emergent power of an organized working class. The ideas reviewed in this chapter come from the domain of the 'social market economy', of the non-totalitarian third way, in its different forms in the post-Second World War period.

We must not forget that there is another third way, the corporatist forms of fascism. While we might easily dismiss the lunacies of Hitlerian Nazism, the originally entirely non-racist fascism of Mussolini, and perhaps even more of José Antonio Primo de Rivera (as expressed through the philo-sophical doctrines of Giovanni Gentile) represented a programme for a non-democratic collectivist order which the interwar Catholic Church generally endorsed. We do not need to consider these approaches here because they are really very peripheral to contemporary social politics, but we have to note them. What we shall examine in detail is the convergence of Keynesian/Collectivist Liberal, Christian Democratic and non-transformational Social Democratic approaches in a broad rejection of unfettered markets.

Chapter 3 deals with the Marxist account as founded around the notion of exploitation and with its contemporary expression in terms of the under-development of 'the social proletariat'.[6] The separation of classical liberal and social market approaches is a commonplace of discussion of these issues. The introduction of the Marxist critique is an unfashionable reassertion of the traditional alternative to those accounts which both accept the inevitability of the continuation of capitalism as a system. This reflects the intellectual power of the Marxist critique, as it has been developed particularly by C.L.R. James and Raya Dunayevska and those who have been influenced by their ideas, and the considerable role of socialist ideas in the formation of the programmes of European social democracy and even of the UK (Old) Labour Party.[7] The examination here will be of approaches which are founded in principle on the notion of an inherent contradiction of interests between a universal proletariat composed of those who own nothing but their labour, and the capitalists who own the means of production, although some versions have left behind the practical implications which flow from this. Of course this formulation is simplistic and in real historical process things are much more complicated, but the core idea is that if the objectives of solidarity are to be achieved then capitalism will have to become something else not founded around the exploitative wage–labour relationship. The arguments which matter are Menshevik/reformist rather than Leninist/ revolutionary, but the notion of revolution must not be equated with that of *coup d'état*.[8] Transformations can take time, but if things are turned over then what has happened is a revolution.

These three chapters are concerned with ideas as expressed in social politics and policy. They are histories of ideas in reflexive interaction with politics, rather than histories of ideas taken alone. For illustrative purposes I refer to the contemporary social politics of four nation-states, the United States, the UK, France and Poland. The UK has undergone a transformation from classic liberalism to initially liberal and then socialist collectivism and back again, with the explicit endorsement by almost all its political elites of the necessity for a 'flexible' labour market in a competitive globalized world. The USA has a history of movement from classical liberalism to liberal collectivism, followed by a collapse of that liberal collectivism justified both by 'blaming the poor' and by an assertion of the inevitability of 'globalization' and the absolute necessity of labour flexibility. These themes have been reinforced by the communitarian movement's assertion of the responsibilities that the poor owe to the community at large, without much equivalent consideration of the responsibilities owed by the rich. What is also interesting is the revival in the USA of genuine trade unionism based on class perspectives and hostility to the untrammelled reign of capital.

France matters because it is in the somewhat surprising synthesis of social Cathólicism and republicanism in contemporary France that we find the origins of the concern with social exclusion as a central theme of the politics of the European Union, and *pace* Veit-Wilson's accurate understanding of the role that the political elite's use of the 'weak' version of the idea has had as a method of closure, we also find a wide popular endorsement of the strong meaning of the expression. Poland is interesting because its formal politics are largely dominated by two political movements with collectivist commitments and traditions, the Christian Democratic Solidarity and the post-communist social democrats,[9] but at the same time under the influence of global agencies like the International Monetary Fund (IMF) there are strong pressures for the development of flexible labour markets.

Poland is a contested post-soviet system with open and democratic politics embedded in a process of economic transformation which seems to go on separate from the political process itself. The choice of nations/societies has also been dictated by the pragmatic consideration that I know something about them, of course.

Part two begins with a chapter dealing specifically with social dynamics. Chapter 4 is the most theoretical chapter of the book. The novel ideas presented in it are challenging because they are different. It is a matter of thinking in a new way about how things change. The chapter seeks to integrate three strands in contemporary social science. One is the concern with grand transformations in the character of the social order as a whole. This has already been identified here as involving a phase shift, a transformation of kind. The most coherent account of this transition is that provided by regulation theory in its various forms, a school which is also discussed in Chapter 3 as part of the Marxist tradition. Here the focus will be on the implications of a shift from a Fordist to post-Fordist social order, considered explicitly in terms of the language of complex dynamics.

The second strand has already been introduced by citation of Leisering and Walker (1998a). This is an emerging school in social science made possible by the availability of new data sets which describe the trajectories of individuals and households through time. These longitudinal data sets, measures of the experience of people through time rather than of their condition at a point in time, are the product of the macroscopic range of vision of the social order which becomes possible given the data management capacities of contemporary computing resources. They are inherently micro in form. They deal with biographies, although it must be noted that those working with them are well aware that biographies occur within a social order which has its own dynamic of change. However, there has not as yet been a systematic integration of the micro level described by, to use complexity theory's term, these ensembles of biographical trajectories and the macro level of social transformation which is described by ideas like that of a shift from a Fordist to a post-Fordist world. My argument is that such an integration is possible if we draw on the concepts of complexity/chaos theory and in particular on Reed and Harvey's (1996) very fruitful notion of nested systems. The last strand in Chapter 4 will provide a summary introduction to these concepts (see Byrne 1998 for a fully developed account) as applied to a consideration of social exclusion. I am convinced that future discussions of social issues will always be dynamic and optimistic in that I believe that the tools of complexity/chaos theory do provide us, not with an elite technology of social engineering, but with a social science which can be applied as part of a programme of dialogical learning and social transformation.[10]

The remainder of Part two draws more extensively on empirical materials and does so with an absolute emphasis on the dynamics of social change, again using illustrations from the USA, the UK, France and Poland. Chapters 5 and 6 deal respectively with the dynamics of income and exclusion and the dynamics of space and exclusion. In both chapters considerable emphasis is placed on the constitutive role of social policies in the creation of the contemporary forms of social division. In other words changes in the whole social order should not be understood as comprising two separate domains of 'economic change' (the organization of production and private consumption) on the one hand and 'policy change' (the organization of collective social reproduction) on the other, with the former being autonomous and proactive and the social domain representing reactive policy responses to the changes which are generated by economic transformation. On the contrary it is argued that the general contemporary character of economic and market relations, which is described using Nelson's (1995) conception of 'post-industrial capitalism', would not be possible without crucial changes in the character of social policies from the form which such policies had during most of the post-Second World War period.

The two areas of dynamic change which are considered in these chapters are respectively changes in the social distribution of incomes taken together with the form of individual/household life term income trajectories, and changes in the socio-spatial organization of urban life, here with an emphasis on the dynamics of neighbourhoods within urban systems and of individuals/ households around urban space over life terms. These two areas have been selected for closer examination because income differentials and spatial segregation are the core focuses of two somewhat separate literatures examining social exclusion and two somewhat separate sets of programmes directed towards its redress.

An examination of income distributions is central to any consideration of processes of change towards or away from equality. Although income is only a proxy for exclusion as a whole, by examining the character of its distribution and changes in the form of its source, which for most people is wage labour or wage substitution benefits, we can get a grip on processes which are central to exclusion considered in relation to exploitation. If we look at potential life course trajectories in terms of both income and its sources, we can start to develop a chaos/complexity founded understanding of the emergent forms of social classes 'in themselves'. Work and wages (and wage substitution and supplementation benefits) do matter a very great deal. We can get a sense of the consequences of social change by looking at these things in some detail.

The examination of exclusion through space is vital for two reasons. First, much of the actual expression of exclusion in urban industrial societies is through spatial segregation. This both defines immediate everyday living conditions and determines, at least in part, subsequent life course trajectories. Such determination is a consequence of differential access to spatially defined collective services and in particular to schools. Second, the restructuring of urban life as a process illustrates very clearly the forms of exclusion from the exercise of power. In post-industrial capitalism the organized working class and its immediate political agents have had the capacity to determine the form of social space taken away from them. It might be argued that this was always a matter of elite determination, rather than of popular planning, although that argument does not hold for the crucial immediate postwar period, but the elimination of social democratic and solidaristic objectives from the planning process matters a very great deal. It also matters that 'inclusion' has become an objective of spatial policy in Europe generally. We need to consider the content of urban initiatives and 'partnerships' rather carefully to find out just what they really involve in terms both of process and of objectives.

In Chapters 4 and 5 'thematics of differentiation' are considered in relation to the processes of exclusion through income and through space. These are class, gender, ethnicity and age. Chapter 4 presents a dynamically founded account of the nature of classes as a set of emergent categories and places considerable emphasis on age, or perhaps more specifically age cohort, as a key determinant control variable for individual trajectories as life courses. Much of the argument and illustration in these two empirical chapters will show that, with two crucial exceptions, the development of the doctrines of possessive individualism in the form of programmes of 'equal *individual* rights' has tended to reduce the significance of income and spatial exclusion around principles of ethnicity and gender. The two exceptions are the position, albeit highly differentiated, of black Americans in the USA, and the position of female single parents and their children, albeit subject to non-linear change, in post-industrial societies in general.

This seems an appropriate point to make it clear that the exclusion which is being examined in this book is internal exclusion within post-industrial societies. It is to do with the consequences of what Madanipour *et al.* (1998) describe in these terms:

> The processes which link the unification of the western European space and the fragmentation of its urban life are complex. At their root, however, is the changing nature of work in contemporary society. Increased global competition leads employers to transfer risks onto the workforce wherever possible. As the balance of employment throughout Europe has shifted from manufacturing to the new service industries the transfer of risk breeds new forms of insecurity among large segments of the workforce, through increasing part-time and temporary working and self-employment, and creates new pressures on household and kinship structures in providing support for their members. As global competitiveness has become the rallying cry of neoliberal governments throughout Europe and as a commitment to the convergence criteria for monetary union has come to be seen as a key element in achieving it, welfare state systems of support for households and individuals are being reconstructed in order to reduce public expenditure.
>
> (Madanipour *et al.* 1998: 7–8)

Exclusion can be external. It can be to do with keeping other people out of a particular nation or block (Fortress Europe) space. Lister (1998) deals with it almost exclusively in that sense in her book dealing with feminist perspectives on citizenship. The ethnic diversity which is in considerable part produced by immigration and which may be a basis for exclusion will be considered in this book, but the focus is on change within industrial societies, not on their relationship with the non-industrial world.

The countries which have been chosen as illustrative examples for this book are all 'developed'. They are all part of the 'first' or former 'second' worlds of industrial capitalism. If not exactly western centred (although Poles are of course very firm about their historical western status) this choice is none the less of countries of 'the North'. I agree that this is a serious issue but I want to justify the choice in terms of more than convenience. It seems to me that Nigel Harris (1987) is right when he argues that development (combined and uneven of course) is now general as a world process. My view is that these advanced industrial societies in a world now dominated by systems of economic organization, if not always of political form, which they developed in the first place, stand as prefigurative of likely developments on a world scale. Societies with very different origins may move in different directions; there is a real issue about the trajectories available in East Asia in a world informed at least in part by different value systems, although developments in South Korea and Japan certainly suggest that the underlying logic of market capitalism is a determinant of the last instance, which as E.P. Thompson (1975) notes has a habit of arriving. However, this text is (only a little shamefacedly) convergenist in account both in global terms and in terms of the likely convergence of existing industrial capitalisms. I shall not neglect the South entirely. On the contrary, one set of ideas to which I shall turn are an absolute product of the South – Freire's ideas about empowerment.

In the conclusion, the themes identified are drawn together with special reference to the potential that exists for the development of both a social politics and a set of social policies which might eliminate social exclusion. The combination of the expressions 'social politics' and 'social policy' is quite deliberate. The argument will be that there are no simple technical fixes to these issues. What is required is a new form of social politics which is founded in a recognition that at the least there are competing social interests at stake here, and that those interests may very well be irreconcilable. This is not just a matter of objectives. It is also a matter of process. In the conclusion I draw on the ideas of Freire as a starting point for thinking about how such a set of processes might be developed in a way which allows for a real partnership between an engaged social science and those who are affected by the process of exclusion in consequence of the transition to post-industrialism.

 **PART ONE**

The possessive individualists: blaming the poor

when we see the lower classes of English people uniformly
singled out as marks for the malice or servility of a certain
description of writers – when we see them studiously
separated like a degraded *caste*, from the rest of the community,
with scarcely the attributes and faculties of the species allowed
them, – nay, when they are thrust lower in the scale of
humanity than the same classes of any other nation in Europe
. . . when we see the *redundant population* (as it is fashionably
called) selected as the butt for every effusion of paltry spite,
and as the last resource of vindictive penal statutes, – when
we see every existing evil derived from this unfortunate race,
and every possible vice ascribed to them – when we are
accustomed to hear the poor, the uninformed, the friendless,
put, by tacit consent, out of the pale of society – when their
faults and wretchedness are exaggerated with eager impatience,
and still greater impatience is shown at every expression of a
wish to amend them – when they are familiarly spoken of as
a sort of vermin only fit to be hunted down, and exterminated
at the discretion of their betters: – we know pretty well what
to think, both of the disinterestedness of the motives which
give currency to this jargon, and of the wisdom of the policy
which should either sanction, or suffer itself to be influenced
by its suggestions.

(Hazlitt 1982 [1821]: 466, original emphases)

William Hazlitt was writing against capital punishment – against a method
for the elimination of the 'useless' poor – which took the form in principle

of suspending them from the neck until dead for stealing goods worth more than a shilling. In practice most were got rid of by geographical separation through transportation, a process responsible not only for the origins of many contemporary Australians but also for most of the White Anglo-Saxon Protestant bloodlines in the American South, and hence for many of the proponents of the contemporary versions of the doctrines of which Hazlitt so disapproved. In the world Hazlitt was denouncing, the poor were punished not only for crime derived from poverty in the first instance, and especially for collective action or even combination directed at resisting poverty, but also, and especially after the establishment of the New Poor Law of 1834, for the very fact of being poor and dependent itself.

Inglis (1972) has pointed out that the establishment of the regime of less eligibility – poor relief in the workhouse was to be 'less eligible', that is worse, than the condition of the 'meanest employed labourer' – was opposed, not only by popular movements which were to develop into the Chartists, but also at an intellectual level by proto-Keynesians like Whately, the Protestant Archbishop of Dublin and main architect of the interventionist report of the Irish Poor Law Commissioners of 1837.[1] However, the combination of an acceptance of Malthus's warning of the implications of a reproducing poor with the utilitarian and market logic not so much of Adam Smith, as of Bentham and Ricardo, led to the establishment of public policies which denied the poor the notion of any social rights (beyond minimal and punitive maintenance), which could be separated from the obligation to work if able for whatever wages the labour market would provide. As Ricardo put it:

> The population can only be repressed by diminishing the encouragement to its *excessive* increase – by leaving contracts between the poor and their employers perfectly free, which would limit the quantity of labour in the market to the effective demand for it. By engaging to feed all who may require food you in some measure create an unlimited demand for human beings, and if it were not for the bad administration of the poor laws, for the occasional hardheartedness of their overseers and the avarice of parishes, which in a degree checks their evil effects, the population and the rates would go on increasing in a regular progression till the rich were reduced to poverty, and till there would no longer be any distinction of ranks.
>
> (quoted in Inglis: 1972: 187, original emphasis)

These origins of such approaches lie with what MacPherson (1962) has called the political doctrine of possessive individualism. This principle, originating in the ideas of Locke, provides a coherent rationale for the rights of individuals both to control their own persons and to possess their own distinctive and private property. It is the foundation of liberalism as a component of modernity and was of the greatest significance for both the American and French revolutions in politics and for the development of the ideological content of political economy as a set of economic doctrines.

Note that it is inherently anti-collectivist. It is a principle directly set against both the estate-based conception of hierarchical natural orders which preceded it, and which it was instrumental in destroying, and the collectivist conceptions of universal human solidarity which inform the socialist and social Christian doctrines which emerged in response to it.

The late eighteenth and early nineteenth centuries in the UK were a crucial period and place for the development of social ideas which retain, or perhaps it is more correct to say have regained, enormous salience in the 1990s. In addition to the general doctrine of possessive individualism, there was the social demography of Malthus with its prediction that population would grow geometrically while resources would increase only arithmetically. We must never forget that the United Kingdom of this period included what is now the Republic of Ireland. In 1841 one-third of the UK's population was Irish. The Irish experience seemed to represent the practical illustration of the problems of too many people and no use for them. Even the socially conscious and proto-Keynesian Irish Commissioners on the Poor Law had no solution to the problems posed for Ireland's development by this excessive population and its political and social response to dispossession of land tenure, than to propose subsidized emigration to the 'empty' colonies. The idea of a useless surplus is one of the most dangerous of all social propositions.

It is particularly dangerous when it is associated with the assignation of moral turpitude and worthlessness to the apparently surplus poor. English studies tend to forget that in the nineteenth century, while Ireland was a colonized society on which English institutions could be imposed, Scotland was a free partner with a different legal code and civil society. The quite distinctive Scottish Poor Law was profoundly influenced by the Calvinistic doctrine of predestination in which the elect of God are separated from those who on the day of judgement will be cast into the outer darkness. It is a doctrine without sympathy for the poor; they deserve everything which they get because it reflects their sinful and depraved state. Classical political economy in its pure form is a remarkably nonjudgemental, if always harsh, doctrine. When it has added to it the moral judgements of the most individualistic forms of Protestantism then insult is added to injury. It is this combination which underpins what might otherwise be seen as the fundamentally contradictory neo-Conservative position. The doctrines of possessive individualism here do not lead to a libertarian absence of judgement as with the utilitarian conception that the poor have to 'stand by their accidents and suffer for the greater general good' but that their poverty is an accident, not something derived from their inherent worthlessness. For the neo-Conservatives the poor deserve everything they get.

In post-industrial capitalism, classical liberalism founded on the doctrine of possessive individualism has experienced a remarkable resurgence. For example MacKay (1998) has remarked that what he calls 'counter-revolutionary economics' (i.e. anti-Keynesian developments since the 1970s) regards unemployment as a choice:

Unemployment as choice places the emphasis on the individual. The unemployed can find a way into work by demonstrating a willingness to accept lower wages, less attractive working conditions, longer journeys to work or by transferring to other occupations, industries and locations. Insufficient flexibility results in unemployment 'by choice'. The counter-revolution represents the relationship between employer and employee as remarkably shallow. The loss of job security for an individual, the loss of a way of life for a community are depoliticised and described in a way that minimises their consequences. Unemployment is seen as a voluntary choice or as the result of government policies that provide incentives to workers to remain unemployed.

(MacKay 1998: 50–1)

There is an absolute and essential continuity between such positions and those of 'godless economics', the 'dismal science' of political economy as it was developed in the Britain in the late eighteenth and early nineteenth centuries culminating in the position expressed by Ricardo. Silver (1994) has described this general form of understanding as one characterized by explanations of poverty/social exclusion which are founded in a doctrine of 'specialization':

In Anglo-American liberalism, exclusion is considered a consequence of *specialisation*: of social differentiation, the economic division of labour and the separation of spheres. It assumes that individuals differ, giving rise to specialisation in the market and in social groups. It is thus individualist in method, although causation is situated not simply in individual preferences but also in the structures created by co-operating and competing individuals – markets, association and the like. Liberalism, thus conceives of the social order, like the economy and politics, as networks of voluntary exchanges between autonomous individuals with their own interests and situations.

(Silver 1994: 542, original emphasis)

It is very important to realize that these ideas not only exist as technical propositions in welfare economics but also are asserted as the basis of a liberal political philosophy founded around the concept of negative freedom. This expression is due to Berlin (1969), who defined negative liberty in terms of freedoms of the individual from coercion and constraint, contrasting this with positive liberty which was about 'freedom to', that is the collective provision of resource systems which extend the role of social action of individuals who would otherwise be constrained. The main exponent of the necessity for the prioritizing of negative freedom in the post-Second World War years was Hayek (1944) with his assertion that collective interventions, originating in the social programmes of the Christian and social democratic and collectivist liberal (Keynesian) positions represented 'the road to serfdom'. A key, and extreme, proponent of the position is Nozick (1974) who would agree with, and was perhaps the source of, Margaret

Thatcher's notorious assertion that: 'There is no such thing as society, only individuals and families'.

It is important to distinguish the arguments of those who argue for unfettered markets and absence of individual constraints on the basis of optimizing efficiency, the technical approach characterizing for example the work of Milton Friedman (1982), from those like Nozick (1974) who assert the absolute primacy of negative liberty. The first category are essentially utilitarians. They accept the 'illfares' of some in order that the total of human welfare may, as they assert, be maximized – the greatest good – although not necessarily calculated to be of the greatest number – this is a programme of overall maximization without regard to any distributive effects. The second are individualists in an essentialist way. Their ethical commitment is anti-collectivist because they assert that anything else diminishes the value of the individual self.

Hazlitt got this crew's number the first time around. Thorstein Veblen (1908) handled their early twentieth-century acolytes with equal panache and severity. His comment on the academic theorization of this position – 'Nowhere is there a sustained inquiry into the dynamic character of the changes which have brought the present (deplorable) situation to pass, nor into the nature and trend of the forces at work in the development that is going forward in this situation' (Veblen 1972 [1908]: 176) – will serve just as well for the 'scientific' economic element in the position now as it did when it was written in 1908.

I want to assert the essentially inseparable character of the three elements of this position. We cannot separate the absolute emphasis on individual freedoms from economic restrictions imposed by the collectivity, from the notion that developments which result from the operation of markets may engender a surplus and unnecessary population. Equally inherent is the moralist condemnation of the poor which derives from Calvinism. Paulin (1998) has reminded us of Hazlitt's political radicalism and that this was founded in a theological Unitarianism which rejected absolutely the notion of singular and selfish salvation – the covenant of faith. Outside the US Bible Belt there are few theological exponents of the covenant of faith today, but Mrs Thatcher's atheistic Protestantism reflected it rather well.

In contemporary Anglo-American social thought these notions of blame and exclusion have become crystallized around the related conceptions of the 'underclass' and 'benefit dependency' and constitute the core of the neo-conservative position on social issues in general. These ideas are not merely intellectual abstractions. They inform public policies, and in particular policies directed at forcing those dependent on state benefits 'from welfare into work' – the current programme of UK 'New Labour'. The next section of this chapter is devoted to an elaboration of these crude perspectives, which must be contrasted with Oscar Lewis's (1966) subtle original conception of the idea of a culture of poverty which we consider in Chapter 5. We then turn to a consideration of the way in which contemporary Anglo-American conceptions of citizenship are inherently individualistic in form.

This individualism can also be clearly identified in the nostrums of the new communitarian movement as propounded by Etzioni (1995) and a review of the approaches suggested under that conception will complete our consideration of these doctrines.

Residuums, underclasses and redundant populations

There is nothing new about the idea of an 'underclass'. MacNicol (1987) points out that: 'versions of the general concept of an inter-generational "underclass" have figured prominently in social debates during the past one hundred years' (1987: 293). Different terms have been used at different times. The commonest nineteenth-century expression was 'residuum' and the idea of a group that has been somehow left behind is an important component of all versions of the idea. The associated idea of a cycle of deprivation in which disadvantage is transmitted from generation to generation has been expressed in both genetic and cultural terms, although it is important to realize that the idea of an underclass can be expressed without reference to either. The term's recent reappearance comes from debates in the USA which to a considerable degree are simply a continuation of the debate about 'cultures of poverty' which began in the aftermath of the Moynihan (1965) report. The main referent for the notion of culture of poverty was the work of Lewis (1966), although most of those who picked up the idea failed to pay any attention to the role that Lewis assigned to culture as a resource of the poor. The concept has become a central part of the intellectual armoury of the American New Right, or at least of the dominant neo-conservative tradition in the New Right, notably in the work of Murray (1984, 1990).

Murray echoed the arguments of Ricardo in terms of the account of the genesis of the 'underclass'. He asserted the role of available welfare benefits in promoting a culture of dependency. Young women 'settled down' as dependants on state benefits available to lone mothers and raised successor generations acculturated to behave in the same way. The account was originally racialized largely by implication – a disproportionate number of lone welfare mothers were black. Murray was brought over to the UK in 1989 by the *Sunday Times* newspaper and in 1990 the right wing think-tank, the Institute of Economic Affairs (IEA), published his account together with a number of criticisms of it. Other texts in the same vein are those published by the 'ethical socialist' Dennis (1997; Dennis and Erdos 1992). These seek to provide a UK-based evidential basis for the view that inadequate parenting, and in particular the absence of respectable fathers, is the causal element in a life course of deprivation and deviance.[2]

The US debate about the underclass has largely been concerned with the position of Afro-Americans in cities. The arguments of the New Right have not gone unchallenged. In particular Wilson (1987, 1989, 1992) and his co-workers have reiterated the criticism that Valentine (1967) made of simplistic versions of the notion of 'culture of poverty' and have pointed out that different behaviour can be explained by constraints without any need for recourse to cultural accounts:

> if the concept of underclass is used, it must be a structural concept: it must denote a new socio-spatial patterning of class and racial domination, recognisable by the unprecedented concentration of the most socially excluded and economically marginal members of the dominated racial and economic group. It should not be used to designate a new breed of individuals moulded freely by a mythical and all powerful culture of poverty.
>
> (Wacquant and Wilson 1989: 25)

I want to return to Wilson's work in Chapter 6 when we examine the dynamics of spatial change because his account is exactly one which assigns causality to the way deindustrialization and associated processes are expressed through the genesis of spatial differentiation. What is important to note here is the emergent rather than nominalist character of Wacquant and Wilson's account. They are not dealing with individual status but with a social collectivity which is more than the sum of the individuals who make it up.

The significance of the notion of surplus population is enormous. We find it recurring in the oddest locations in contemporary thought. For example Bauman (1998), whose account is dealt with in Chapter 3 because it is founded around a rejection of the idea that the poor form a meaningful reserve army for production, regards the 'New Poor' as surplus both for purposes of production and consumption. This designation of people as 'useless' matters. The classical liberal position does not judge that uselessness. The neo-conservatives equate uselessness with worthlessness. Indeed they have a theory of causation for such worthlessness. It is self-inflicted through the intergenerational transmission of 'the culture of poverty' and consequent habits of 'welfare dependency'.

In Chapter 6 we consider the sociological account of the notion of a culture of poverty as an emergent form, which originates with the work of Oscar Lewis (1966). In his formulation the idea is subtle and important. However, here I want to deal with the use made of the notion of a 'culture of poverty' when the poor's own attitudes and values are identified as the source of their poverty in a process of blaming them for their own condition – the contemporary version of Protestantism's excluded and morally deficient non-elect. Lawrence Mead (1988), perhaps the most important US neo-conservative, has argued in terms which are foundational to the counter-revolution in economic theory, that the condition of the poor derives in large part from their obdurate refusal of 'poor work'. Poor citizens, as opposed to immigrants, argue that they want to work but they refuse to take low paid and unpleasant work, demanding instead 'decent' or 'proper' jobs. In consequence they fail to obtain any sort of work record and cannot gain access to reasonable work on the basis of proven work commitment.

Their failures become internalized and lead to apathy and defeatism. That this approach assumes no discontinuity, no barriers of kind, between 'poor work' and 'decent work' should be obvious. We shall see in subsequent chapters that such an assumption is wholly wrong.

Mead asserts that his own approach is that of non-moralist utilitarianism and that the policy proposals which flow from it are essentially behaviourist rather than judgemental. In other words the task of public policy is to create incentive systems, with the incentives being both positive carrots and negative sticks, which make work preferable to benefit dependency. However, a moment's reflection on the moral element, which seems inseparable from any programme that sees the problem in terms solely of individual behaviour, suggests that this economistic rationalizing is disingenuous. Only professional economists and policy wonks ever confine themselves to a rationalist account of individual poverty, and not even all of them. In the hands of politicians we always get the moral argument, the judgement of the poor as unworthy, if perhaps redeemable, sinners.

Citizenship?

citizenship is a strategically important concept *intellectually*, not least in Sociology and Social Theory. It is important in principle because it provides a common field (1) for the sociological study of society to meet the study of social policy and politics and (2) for social theory to meet explicitly normative analysis in political theory and moral philosophy.
(Roche 1992: 2, original emphasis)

For many years T.H. Marshall's (1950) discussion of citizenship was not an important theme in sociology or political theory. Rather reference to it was characteristic of courses in social administration where the kind of liberal political theory which underpins the idea was seen as representing the philosophical contribution to the study of the field of social policy. Marshall's account is one of an evolutionary development of the defined rights of individuals expressed in terms of individual persons acquiring progressively judicial, political and social rights. It is an account founded in a Whig history style interpretation of the development of the social politics of modernity.

From the point of view of those who espouse theories of possessive individualism, Marshall's account is inherently contradictory. There is no problem with judicial rights. Indeed the existence of such rights and of mechanisms for their enforcement, including the enforcement of rights derived from processes of contract, are central to any programme based on negative conceptions of liberty. Democratic rights are more tendentious, although few now publicly argue that they should be available only to those who possess a property based stake in the social order, whatever they may say in abstract discussion and do in terms of the operations of the mechanisms of the state. It is the social rights, certainly components of 'positive liberty', which are dismissed by those arguing from a classical liberal position, because they inevitably involve claims made through political mechanisms which challenge the property rights of others.

Given this, it may seem surprising that I have chosen to discuss citizenship in a chapter which deals essentially with ideas and principles which have their origin in the individualistic tradition of nineteenth century political economy. After all Marshall's framework is one shaped absolutely by the character of universalist social service provision through a tax based welfare state in the UK after 1945. That is certainly the context of the development of the account, but I want to argue, first, that the approach is not actually one founded in a universalist programme but rather represents a traditional gloss placed on events which were not the product of actions of the elite who had the privilege of describing them, and second, that the major trend in late twentieth century discussions of citizenship has abandoned the collectivist element which was inherent in the context in which Marshall developed the idea. Citizenship, and its derivative communitarianism, are merely general social programmes derived from the doctrines of possessive individualism and negative liberty. They are an intellectual accommodation with the necessity for social arrangements, but they remain inherently antisocial (in both the sociological and popular sense of that word) at the core.

To understand the significance of the historical context of Marshall's ideas we have to consider the anomalous character of the UK welfare state. Esping-Andersen's (1990) typology of welfare regimes is of very considerable value. However, this typology describes the institutional character of welfare systems, rather than the processes by which those welfare systems were created. Indeed it might be characterized as a typology in which institutional form predominates as a demarcating characteristic, but considerable attention is also given to the dominant motifs of intellectual debate in the literature surrounding the institutional forms.

Esping-Andersen had considerable difficulty locating the UK in his typology. In some respects the levels of welfare provision were not high, but there was a universalist free at the point of need National Health Service (NHS) – a massively important representation of what Westergaard (1995) described as the expression of a 'welfare aim beyond the market'. This is not a residual welfare state, neither is it the welfare state to be found under conditions of accommodation between catholic social teaching and civic republicanism. Rather it is a welfare state created by working-class social democracy but profoundly influenced in its development by new collectivist liberalism. If subsequent debate about its character and future has been largely conducted between collectivist and classical (free market) liberals, with a period of structuralist Marxist ranting to add spice, the relative silence of a social democratic voice does not mean that the thing being discussed is not inherently social democratic in character. Indeed Esping-Andersen explicitly endorses the view that the system immediately post implementation represented a high point of democratic socialist achievement in terms of decommodification (1990: 53–4).

My argument is that the welfare state in the UK was created by ordinary people through what Williams (1962) called *The Long Revolution*, a process of political, cultural and social action. The academic discussion of these issues, particularly by political philosophers, has in effect stolen that act of creation from the people who made it happen. These approaches ignore in particular the social consciousness, as developed by wartime experiences, which was the origin of Labour's 1945 victory and of the universalist welfare state. There is ample evidence in the reports of mass observation of the character of social views in this period. Even that elitist (if radical) Liberal, Beveridge felt obliged, or perhaps to be fair 'able' is a better word, to end his *Full Employment in a Free Society* with the exhortation:

> The British people can win full employment while remaining free . . . But they have to win it, not wait for it. Full employment, like social security, must be won by a democracy; it cannot be forced on a democracy or given to a democracy. It is not a thing to be promised or not promised by a Government, to be given or withheld from Olympian height. It is something that the British democracy should direct its Government to secure, at all costs save the surrender of the essential liberties. Who can doubt that full employment is worth winning, at any cost less than surrender of those liberties? If full employment is not won and kept, no liberties are secure, for to many they will not seem worth while.
>
> (Beveridge 1944: 258)

The problem is that citizenship has been formulated as a concept almost entirely in terms of abstract philosophical discussion rather than by reference to the real historical social politics, the long revolution, which created its modern form. It is this stripping out of the history which has made possible the appropriation of what can be a transformational and collectivist conception by proponents of possessive individualism.

It is important to note that this critique does not apply to Marshall himself. On the contrary he belongs within the intellectual and political tradition which can be dated in the UK from the Newcastle programme of the Liberal Party in the 1890s, when the original ideological foundations of that party in free market individualism were replaced by an accommodating collectivism drawing on Collingwood and the English Hegelians for its intellectual provenance. This was the mind set of Beveridge and Keynes, as well as of Marshall, and we shall consider it in Chapter 2. Turner (1993) describes the original conception thus:

> In the work of Marshall, the concept was developed to answer a problem in liberalism. In capitalism, liberal values were successful in emphasising freedoms and individualism, but there was no easy answer to critics who pointed out that the classic freedoms . . . were ineffective tokens for the majority of the population who lived in poverty. In part, the institutions of citizenship, especially in the British case, functioned

to ameliorate the condition of the working class without transforming the entire property system. While 'citizenship' functions as a description of certain institutions, it covertly carries the implication that they *ought* to exist in the interests of social harmony.

(Turner 1993: 176–7, original emphasis)

It is the dominant contemporary 1990s usage of citizenship which is individualistic to the core. Jordan (1996) expresses this well when he dismisses 'the analysis of poverty and social exclusion in terms of citizenship, especially within the liberal tradition' because of

the narrow focus of this concept on individual rights and responsibilities, at the expense of interdependency and collective action. Indeed the whole debate about 'social citizenship' has been largely directed into this cul-de-sac – the search for a 'balance' between rights and responsibilities conceived as formal reciprocities between individual members of market oriented systems.

(Jordan 1996: 85)

It has to be said that citizenship expressed in these sorts of terms is a profoundly unsociological idea. It is a micro-theory which essentially ignores the macro-structures, the social order, within which citizenship as a practice must be embedded. There is one sociological proposition of the New Right which must be exempted from that criticism. It is perhaps most coherently expressed by Saunders (1993) when he asserts:

most people today enjoy much higher real household incomes such that they can afford to buy many of the items which would have been out of their reach in the nineteenth century . . . A move to privatized consumption does not therefore signal a move back to mass poverty and deprivation.

(Saunders 1993: 64)

This is an absolute standard argument. If minimum standards are high enough in absolute terms, then whatever the inequalities that may exist in relative terms, there is no longer any need for collectivist intervention which impinges on negative liberty. This kind of argument implicitly incorporates a crude version of the view, much more coherently expressed by Eder (1993) that the rise in overall real living standards (for Eder among other factors) not only has eliminated any social justice case for major redistributive intervention in the name of citizenship, but also has eliminated the causal processes which created an emergent and self-conscious class-based collective politics demanding such redistribution. However, at least we have sociology here.

Absolutist liberals have the virtue of logical consistency in their views on these matters. Neo-conservatives are inherently inconsistent. Roche (1992) summed up the neo-conservative dilemma in these terms:

Neoconservatism is to a considerable extent ambiguous and incoherent in its conception of the poor and underclass citizen as simultaneously capable of moral reform by authoritarian reminders about duty *and* socially incompetent and psychologically incapable of rational self-control and thus of consistent moral action . . . Overall probably the major underlying weakness in the neo-conservative challenge to the dominant paradigm has been its inability to connect systematically its two main values. On the one hand it supports 'morality' and 'traditional' patriarchal, familistic and 'work ethic' morality in particular. On the other, it supports capitalism as an economic system, which is arguable inherently anti-traditional.

(Roche 1992: 49 original emphasis)

There is an important additional contradiction here. Neo-conservatism asserts a work ethic but cannot assert a right, as opposed to a duty, to work, precisely because full employment recasts the basis of the relationship between labour and capital around the wage relationship. The reserve army, capitalism must always have with it.

Communitarianism has been proposed as a way of resolving the crucial problem for neo-conservatives of reconciling the idea of rights for individuals with obligations which those individuals may owe to the wider collectivity. The most important formulation of the idea is that proposed by Etzioni (1995). It is very important to distinguish this sort of argument from the organic approaches which will be the subject of Chapter 2. The account of communitarianism as presented by the US originating political movement of that name is one firmly grounded in the tradition of possessive individualism, even if the core of the approach is based around an assertion of the need to move back from a social order characterized by excessive individualism founded on an overgenerous interpretation of personal rights.

There is a deal of confusion in the account but it hinges around a kind of reverse principle of subsidiarity, of the Catholic doctrine that functions should be handed down below the level of the state to that level of social organization which is best fitted to their execution. Catholic organicism works down from the universal. Communitarianism works up from the individual. It does of course challenge the notion of the ultimate sovereignty of the individual through its imposition of community ordered moral and civic obligations but it does so in relation to an undifferentiated conception of the character of citizens. For example Etzioni (1995) calls for a moratorium on the 'manufacturing of new rights' and is scathing about the 81 per cent of Americans (US citizens I assume he means) who regard health care as a right and the 66 per cent who likewise see decent housing as a right, asking 'who will pay for unlimited health care and adequate housing for all?' (Etzioni 1995: 5). The answer could well be all the rich who have benefited so massively out of the existing systems, including *inter alia* the grossly overpaid US medical profession by reducing their incomes to approximately those of physicians in other advanced industrial countries, the owners of capital in unnecessary private health insurance companies by introducing an efficient single purchaser model on Canadian lines (no radical socialism like the UK NHS), and the exploitative rich in general by (a) paying their taxes at all and (b) paying more in taxes. In other words the possessive individualistic origins of communitarianism presumptively, if not absolutely, leave intact the very tightly possessed property rights of those who have them, regardless of the consequences for the fabric of the social order. They readily impose obligations of behaviour on the poor but there is no equivalent discussion of the obligations of the rich. Potter of Bedford Falls in Frank Capra's *It's a Wonderful Life* (1946) is not the problem for the communitarians. It is the poor who must be made to behave.

In the UK typical contemporary proponents of this sort of stuff are Dennis (1997) and Green (1996, 1998). Green states his position thus:

> if too many people look to the government for the means of life, then this dependency has harmful effects which accumulate over time. The initial harm results from people organising their affairs so that they qualify for benefit. Having crossed the boundary between independent self-support and reliance on the work of others, individuals are inclined to neglect friendships or relationships with people who could provide a helping hand in a spirit of mutual respect. Because their self-respect diminishes, they often become more shameless in their determination to live at the expense of others. They also fail to join organisations like churches or voluntary associations, where they would meet people who would gladly provide temporary restorative help. As a further consequence, they acquire fewer skills of co-operating with others, and face fewer challenges. In turn, they have fewer opportunities to strengthen their characters by overcoming adversity. As a result, they are more prone to manipulation by politicians, some of whom are only too willing to 'buy' their votes with promises of 'more'. Politicians whose model of society is one of leaders and led are very happy to preserve in being a section of the population that will trade its votes for cash rewards.
>
> (Green 1998: vii)

The reality is that far from the poor being a constituency of politicians in the UK and even more in the USA, they are now so alienated from a political process which seems to disregard them as a significant social group, that they increasingly don't vote in the former state and don't really vote at all in the latter. However, it is the 'moral' fault argument which is central to Green's position.

These kinds of accounts are the 'moralistic' and 'astructural' version of communitarianism. Küng (1997) describes them exactly:

> moralism and moralizing overvalue morality and ask too much of it. Why? Moralists make morality the sole criterion for human action and ignore the relative independence of various spheres of life like economics, law and politics. As a result they tend to absolutize intrinsically justified

norms and values (peace, justice, environment, life, love) and also to exploit them for the particular interests of an institution (state, party, church, interest group). Moralism manifests itself in a one-sided and penetrating insistence on particular moral positives (for example, in questions of sexual behaviour) which make a rational dialogue with those of other convictions impossible.

(Küng 1997: xiv–xv)

There is one further topic which we must consider before we leave the doctrines founded in individualism. It is the inherent tension between an economic system founded on possessive individualism and ordered through free markets on the one hand, and democratic majority government, especially when informed by the principle of subsidiarity, on the other. Crouch and Marquand (1989) put this rather well:

> One of the central assumptions of the new right is that choice is max-imised through the market, not through politics: that the frictionless, undisturbed market is a realm of freedom and the polity a realm of domination and manipulation. Grant that and it follows logically that the sphere of the political should be curtailed; one obvious way to do this is to limit the scope of subordinate political authorities. On new right assumptions, provided people have the chance to vote in national elections and to participate in open political discussion and lobbying, they should find variety, choice and delegation through market activ-ity alone, and not through further political forms.
>
> (Crouch and Marquand 1989: viii–xi)

The New Right will accept lower level political entities only when these are considered to act as a bastion against the collectivism of a higher level, for example in the way the doctrine of 'states' rights' can be used against what has, since the New Deal, been seen as the collectivist tendency of the federal level in the USA, or the basis of 'Eurosceptic' defence of the UK nation state against the European Union. It is thus adamantinely opposed to the principle of subsidiarity, that is the principle of the necessity for and necessary autonomy of lower spatial levels for the management of political life. Indeed there is a tendency in practice, if not much these days in formal principled expression, for New Right politics to revert to the conception that citizenship rights of political determination are only available to those with property. This is the effective situation in the USA given the priv-ileged position of campaign donors and the mass abstention of the poor.

The argument of this chapter was stated at the beginning of industrial capitalism by Hazlitt. The political and social doctrines, and the accounts of the social order which are coloured by them, which flow from possessive individualism and the division of people into the worthy and the depraved, serve particular and restricted material interests. They are ideological in essence. All political and social doctrines serve interests. The issue is whether those interests are particular or universal – or at the very least of the relative size of the interests served. All social accounts are ideologically coloured. However, the realist position which informs this book does not accept that all accounts are merely expressions of interests – this is not a postmodernist text. We can establish how things are – there is a truth to be got at. In Chapters 5 and 6 we shall try to do that. In Chapters 2 and 3 we turn to two other sets of doctrines, recognizing always that the distinction between social doctrine and account of the social is simply heuristic, which are certainly different from each other, but which do share an essential commitment to the social and collective as the foundation of any social politics.

Order and solidarity:
collectivist approaches

harmony and justice stem from the recognition that persons
have a fundamental dignity of their own since they are
made in God's image, independently of course of what they
achieve or fail to achieve (and independently of course of
their productivity!). Thus, the whole community shares
the responsibility for meeting the basic needs of each of its
members, while each of its members accepts his or her own
responsibility for contributing to the common good of all . . .
Such a community is incompatible with unbridled individualism,
which in the name of freedom allows inequitable access to
material and human resources. It is also incompatible with an
unchecked collectivism, which in the name of equality and
the good of the majority exercises an evermore rigid control
over the thoughts and actions of its members. Neither
freedom nor equality represent an absolute value. Both need
to be set within the context of fraternity, which stresses the
givenness of mutual belonging as prior to any relationship
based solely on shared interests.

> (Baelz 1984, quoted in Council of Churches for
> Great Britain and Ireland (CCBI) 1997: 2–3)

This chapter examines the intellectual origins and contemporary form of an
internally varied set of social ideas or programmes which can none the less
be distinguished from those reviewed in Chapter 1 by the emphasis which
they place on the significance of the collective, on the importance of the social
order as a whole, and on the obligations which all members of the collectivity
owe to that social order. However, although the positions reviewed here

share the collectivist objectives of the Marxist position, the subject of Chapter 3, they can be distinguished from even the most reformist versions of Marxism by their belief that the capitalist social order can deliver in terms of collective social goals. For the exponents of these positions, market capitalism must be corrected by political action but it is a corrigible system.

Of particular importance is the implication of these ideas for the direction of the conduct of governance, for the specification of the objectives of public administration and economic management at the macro level, whether that macro level is that of nation-state, transnational block, or world system as a whole. We should also note, as Baelz (1984) makes clear, that there is an insistence in these perspectives on the value of all individuals. This is not just in relation to their passive right to good treatment, but also within the Judaeo-Christian (and of course Islamic) conception of their creative capacity as being made in the image of God. As we shall see this is usually expressed in relation to ideas about the right to work, but there can be rather more to it.

Of course, we are dealing here with fuzzy sets. Communitarianism in particular represents a set of approaches which provide a bridge between the classical liberal conceptions discussed in Chapter 1 and the positions reviewed here. The boundary must be drawn between 'moral communitarianism' of the kind described in Chapter 1 in which the responsibility is assigned to individuals and 'socio-economic communitarianism' which displays some awareness of the significance of social structures and of the faults of capitalism as a mode of production (see Driver and Martell 1997). Likewise the social democratic tradition links the perspectives presented in this chapter, all of which are characterized by a rejection of the notion that fundamental class conflict is inherent in the capitalist order, to Marxist accounts which do emphasize the reality of such fundamental conflict and its role as the active contradiction of capitalism itself.

None the less a clear distinction can be drawn at both boundaries. The approaches discussed here, including those versions of communitarianism which are not merely moralistic, all agree that market capitalism is an unstable system which requires collective regulation. They all accept that, as Heilbroner (1993) puts it,

> If the great scenarios teach us anything, it is that the problems that threaten capitalism arise from the private sector, not the public. The saturation of demand and the degradation of the labour force that are the great difficulties of Smith's conception; the crises and contradictions of Marx's model; the inability to reach full employment that Keynes selected as the great flaw; the cultural erosion of Schumpeter's scenario – these are all failures that arise from the workings of the capitalist economy, not from any interference with those workings by the polity. What solutions, what counter-measures can there be to problems caused by the private realm except those that originate in the public realm?
>
> (Heilbroner 1993: 112)

In summary we might say that the perspectives outlined in Chapter 1 argue that market capitalism will work well and that the only role of the political systems of the collectivity is to ensure that the recalcitrance of the idle is overcome by appropriate discipline, that the perspectives being reviewed here accept the need for the collective regulation and management of capitalism in order to ameliorate excesses of inequality and maintain stability in an inherently unstable system, but that Marxist socialist perspectives argue that capitalism is not a long term option and that the future sustainability of human societies depends on its transformation into something else, by a process of what may well be a long revolution based on the accretion of the effects of social reform

We have to be careful here because the political forces informed by the conceptions being discussed are currently in a state of crisis about their capacity for maintaining programmes derived from these perspectives against the power of globalized capital. The inherent tension is very evident in the contradictions both within and between the two key European Union White Papers, *European Social Policy: A Way Forward for the Union* (European Commission DGV 1994) and *Growth, Competitiveness, and Employment* (European Commission 1994), and even more so in the treatment of the policy proposals derived from them. These were 'postponed indefinitely' by European Finance Ministers at their 1996 meeting of ECOFIN (the Economics and Finance Council of the Union). Actions like this have led Therborn (1995) to the gloomy conclusion that:

> Unemployment as a specific social problem was intellectually and politically discovered in the early 1890s, during the then Great Depression. For twenty to thirty years – in Scandinavia and Eastern Europe for more than forty years – after World War II, the problem appeared to have been solved. Now a hundred years after its discovery, it seems to be in a process of being accepted as the final verdict of the court of capitalism. Or, in the bulk of Western Advice to the East, presented, *sotto voce*, as something which should be created as a normal part of a market economy.
>
> (Therborn 1995: 58–9)

Walker (1997) takes up this point exactly in relation to the theme of this book:

> It is ironic . . . that European discourse should have alighted on the concept of social exclusion at a time when market trends, including the creation of a single European market and currency, are generalising more inequality and insecurity and there is an apparent loss of support for social protection.
>
> (R. Walker 1997: 49)

There are distinct signs that the political forces founded on the 'non-transformational' collectivisms which are the subject of this chapter, are in danger of giving up on their programme for sustaining an inclusive capitalism in the face of the economic gales, storm force winds and hurricanes of globalization. However, the emerging crisis of the financial basis of that capitalism itself, the chronic overcapacity of manufacturing systems in relation to effective world demand and the instability of secondary property and leisure-based alternatives for investment, is likely to produce a rather rapid return to the first principles which have informed those forces in the past.

We are dealing here with ideas with rather different provenances, Catholic 'solidarism', its mirror image in the solidarism of Jacobin republicanism, non-transformational socialism, and Keynesianism, which came together in the postwar years in western Europe as the basis of a social politics which really is rather well described by the now neglected expression 'social market economy'. The best account of this I have encountered is that offered by the theologian Hans Küng (1997), who locates it in a post-Second World War desire to realize a 'new third form' between the totalitarian controlled economy and the purely liberal market economy. Küng asserts:

> Beyond doubt the social market economy had more realist presuppositions than ultraliberalism, which professed itself to be so realist. After all the fearful experiences of twentieth-century Europe it was not longer possible to maintain the ultraliberal idea that a natural harmony of interests had to be the model for economic and social life. Conflicts, not harmony, are the realistic starting point for the social market economy; to this degree there was an agreement with Marxism. But at the same time there was a concern not to rake up the old 'class struggle' between labour and capital all over again: . . . A positive effect of this was that here ideas of Protestant social ethics were combined with those of Catholic social teaching, the foundations for which were laid in the papal encyclicals *Rerum Novarum* (1891) and *Quadrigesimo Anno*. These had been thought through above all by advocates of the concept of solidarity.
> (Küng 1997: 201–2)

Küng notes that these positions developed an understanding of solidarity and subsidiarity: 'Long before any "communitarianism"' (1997: 202). This really seems to me to be something more than the stock-holding conception of social practice ascribed by Jordan (1996) to the European mercantilist tradition in which the poor are seen as 'more like sheep and cattle to be farmed (regulated and provided for as part of the creation and conservation of national wealth), than wild animals to be tamed' (as in the Anglo-Saxon liberal tradition) (Jordan 1996: 3). It is also qualitatively different from the kind of organicism which is founded on the idea of a social order formed of natural ranks and places to which people are properly allocated, and which sees departure from the allocated places as threatening to the integrity of the whole system. The complex being reviewed here is not really conservative in that sense. It allows for change and indeed regards some change as not only desirable but probably essential.

It certainly has to be distinguished from the version of the term 'third way' presented by British Prime Minister Tony Blair in his speech to the United Nations of September 1998 (Blair 1998). For Blair, as for the Borrie

(1994) chaired Commission on Social Justice before him, the power of global markets is so great that no political system can stand against them. The best it can achieve is tendential modification. The real idea of the third way does not subordinate politics to economics in this way. On the contrary, as French Prime Minister Lionel Jospin does realize, it is precisely founded on the use of state power to regulate economic systems so that they do not challenge social goals.

Silver (1994) argues that 'At the heart of the question "exclusion from what?" lies a more basic one, the problem of social order during times of profound social change in society' (1994: 541). We must remember that the 1990s are by no means the first period in which this question has been asked. Citizens of the Anglo-Saxon democracies live in societies without a twentieth century experience of totalitarianism. This is not true, above all for Germany, and the development of the intellectual foundations of postwar Christian Democracy is far too little appreciated in Anglo-Saxon political thought. In this respect Esping-Andersen's otherwise very useful typologizing of welfare regimes, by the content of their institutional forms, does us a disservice. We are far too likely to see the Bismarckian forms of work-based insurance as somehow representing a simple degree of continuous 'conservative' organic integrationism.

Küng (1997) makes it very clear that the social market economy programme, as developed by Ludwig Erhard in the first twenty years of the Federal Republic, originated in the regulated liberalism of the Freiburg school, 'which called for a strong state capable of establishing an ordered framework for free competition while at the same time pursuing a policy of order to maintain competition' (Küng 1997: 199). The 'order liberals' who pursued these objectives were very different in their approach from the classical liberals whose views were being reasserted by Hayek. They argued for 'the interdependence of society, the state and the economy' (Küng 1997: 200) in marked contrast to the absolute privileging of the market economy which characterizes classic liberalism. At the same time they were also very different in views from the organic totalitarianisms both of the old regimes and of fascism.[1] They were trying to make a non-totalitarian capitalism work, and of course they succeeded for many years.

The interesting thing about the European Christian Democrats, and especially the German Christian Democrats, was the degree to which they combined ideas from an analytical and atheological programme, order liberalism, with the theologically informed account of solidarity which underpinned Catholic social teaching after *Rerum Novarum*. French Republicanism, to the considerable degree that it is inspired by Rousseau's ideas, emphasizes solidarity in terms of integration into the social order to an even greater degree than its old Catholic antagonist, hence the ease with which Gaullism could emerge in postwar France as a reconciliation of Catholic perspectives with a godless republic.

The social democratic case is more complicated. Here we find in Europe two different reconciliations going on. The first is that in French and Belgian socialism of social democratic and Catholic perspectives.[2] The second is in Swedish, German and British socialism of formal socialist objectives with a Keynesian programme of macro-economic management. These combinations had broadly similar objectives but very different mechanisms were to be employed to achieve them.

All organicist programmes revolve around the development of institutions which represent both means for the formal attachment between individuals and the collectivity, and processes through which individuals are integrated culturally into the social order. The German combination of education and social insurance shows this very well. Marris (1996), an unreconstructed Keynesian, sums this up when he remarks:

> Continental Western Europe has indeed suffered severe demand inefficiency in her labour market, caused by inadequate growth, but on the account of the different 'Catholic' social regime (and in Germany especially, educational system) the adverse effects, *rather than as in the UK and USA concentrating on low-eds* (males with minimal educational qualifications) *have spread more evenly over the whole working population.*
> (Marris 1996: 176, original emphases)

The two aspects to this institutional integration need to be spelled out. First, in Germany, high general levels of education meant that most citizens have the qualifications necessary in principle for well paid jobs. As there is insufficient demand for the volume of qualified labour which is made available, then integration is achieved through the institutional mechanism of generous income substitution benefits, the Bismarckian model. This of course suggests that 'Welfare to Work' schemes will not work unless low wages are accepted by workers qualified to levels which would normally command higher wages. It is the failure of the supply side mechanism to achieve solutions – the delivery of highly qualified labour by educational systems does not create employment unless there is demand for the products of that employment – which is the origin of the contemporary crisis in western European welfare systems. Says Law – supply creates its own demand – no more holds good for qualified labour than it does for any other commodity.

This is where the Keynesian perspectives become particularly interesting. They were much discussed in the early 1980s but have almost disappeared from the formal content of contemporary debate. Heald (1983) pointed out that

> The crisis of the Keynesian social democratic state is in essence, the loss of faith in its continuing efficacy as a political accommodation of both universal suffrage and organised labour with a market oriented economy.
> (Heald 1983: 258)

Why should this mechanism which was so successful for so long, have ceased to work? One important explanation for this is basal. The Keynesian programme was implemented in a period when the general level of capital in the economies of the advanced industrial world was low. This applied across a range of spheres. There were deficits in productive capital which reflected the impact of wartime destruction. There were deficits in social capital, particularly in housing and transport infrastructure, which reflected both wartime destruction and the poor quality of social capital developed in the nineteenth century. In addition there was a massive military industrial complex engaged in both a cold war involving competitive technology development and a series of hot post-colonial wars. All this served to maintain global aggregate demand.

The system suffered a severe cost shock in the early 1970s with the very rapid rise in oil prices, which led to a drain of resources outwith the expenditure based demand of the western economies, despite the best efforts of UK, US and French merchants of death to sell weapons systems to the primarily Arab powers now retaining a far greater share of oil revenues. However, the filling up of productive and social capital deficits, coupled with massive productivity gains in manufacturing industries in general, created a situation in which the intrinsic demand for labour weakened in advanced industrial economies. Indeed the key collapse in demand has been that of demand for skilled manual labour. Productivity gains have depended on the replacement of such labour by a combination of machinery and less skilled labour. At the same time the 'product mix' of the global capitalist economy has moved away from the heavy engineering products which were the main locus of skilled manual employment towards both light electronic goods and a range of services. These changes in the nature of the real economy are part of the story of the weakness of classic Keynesian policies since the late 1970s.[3]

Another important factor has been the globalization of finance capital based on new communications technology. For nationally based Keynesian policies to be effective, the political forces vested in nation-states had to be able to control capital flows. After the early 1980s they no longer had the capacity to do this, as was demonstrated by the early failures of François Mitterand's administration in France. Under Thatcher the development of this globalization of finance was of course actively encouraged, even at the meso level of urban planning through the subordination of the planning of London to the City's role as a locus of the global financial markets.

It is conventional to discuss the account of social exclusion offered by the perspectives being reviewed here in terms of the failure of integration, particularly with work but also with general social systems. Martin (1996) describes the French usage of the expression as founded in a fear of 'a double fragility: a fragile integration with the world of work and a fragile connection with a network of family and friends' (Martin 1996: 382). This is certainly part of the story. There is what Levitas (1996) has very appropriately described as a strongly Durkheimian element in the perspectives which characterize the approaches of the middle way. However, her entirely correct emphasis on the significance attached by these perspectives to integration through work – 'integration into society is elided with integration into work' (Levitas 1996: 11) – actually misses the point that this emphasis on work in historical terms has been radical. The idea of a 'right to work' is the project of two political sets which represent a response to the socialist claim for the transformation of society, on the one hand the Keynesian 'bourgeois liberal' – the new order liberalism of the twentieth century, and on the other the Catholic influenced Christian Democrats. I would agree with Levitas's view that, in the contemporary formal political expression of these positions by the European Union,

> The cause of exclusion is not the fundamental nature of capitalism (which never gets discussed) but the 'contemporary economic and social conditions' which tend to exclude some groups from the cycle of opportunities.
>
> (Levitas 1996: 8)

However, the political understandings which underpin Christian Democracy, non-transformational Social Democracy and new Liberalism are all founded in a recognition that there are problems with the fundamental nature of capitalism and with the balance of power within it of labour as against capital. These perspectives come together in an interesting way in the publication of the Council of Churches for Great Britain and Ireland dealing with *Unemployment and the Future of Work* (CCBI 1997) and an exegesis of that text is a good way of illustrating their implications:

> The most fundamental question we have had to address is this: should we still, as church leaders have in the past, argue the case that enough paid work should be created for everyone, or should we adopt a new set of values in the belief that full employment is essentially a thing of the past? . . . We have concluded that the value of work is central to the Christian understanding of the human condition, not an optional extra. Society should not give up on paid work . . . 'Enough good work for everyone' has to become an explicit national aim in its own right . . . The aim of enough good work cannot be allowed to remain a hoped for, but ultimately optional, by-product to economic growth.
>
> (CCBI 1997: 7–8)

The most interesting thing about the above identification of principle is the emphasis not just on work, but on 'good work'. The report defines 'good work' thus:

> Work is rightly seen as a form of service to one another, to the community and to the well-being of the world. All those who are called to such service should accept it. But willing service should never become a kind of servitude. The wish to do useful work, indeed the need to earn a living, should never be exploited by employers offering pay and conditions which are unfair and offensive to human dignity.
>
> (CCBI 1997: 102)

The same point was made by Veit-Wilson's (1998) Dutch informants:

> In The Netherlands, when we consider the social security system norms, we always start by looking at the international treaties we signed, for instance on economic, social and cultural rights. *You* (the British) are always talking about poverty, about an eighteenth or nineteenth century subject. *We* are talking about how we maintain a system where everybody is free to accept suitable labour. That is a political discussion at the moment, of which the main item is, is a citizen able to accept suitable labour and is not *forced* to accept it because he cannot afford to live without suitable labour. So the main political issue has been up to now, is there enough suitable labour for people to enforce the right to gain a living based on free and individual choices? So the discussion then is, what is suitable labour? What kind of norms do we have to guarantee that these people can choose their own labour by free will and are not forced to take any job which turns up? Of course the political question is whether or not the social security burden is too high to give people such freedom.
>
> (Veit-Wilson 1998: 93, original emphases)

The conflation of the views informed by a radical theology with those of conservatism as a single paradigm describing positions on social exclusion is mistaken. Catholic-influenced politics will always have within it a deeply conservative strand which expresses itself as a reactionary organicism. However, this is not informed by the principle of 'solidarity/fraternity'. Rather it revolves around an intrinsically hierarchical conception of proper place. In contrast the principle of 'solidarity/fraternity' is essentially anti-hierarchical. Silver (1994) does recognize this as a possibility:

> Although organicism is often considered conservative, these paradigms may in fact call for state intervention to restructure the established society and institute changes in pursuit of social justice. Thus, organicism and Catholicism in a context of entrenched privilege may actually be radical.
>
> (Silver 1994: 546)

In reality this kind of synthesis of spiritual solidarity and revolutionary fraternity is inherently radical. It is probably a key element in the formation of potential coalitions for social change. We can see this by attempting to consider what these perspectives make of the idea of 'citizenship' and the remainder of this chapter will be devoted to that task.

Citizenship considered from a solidaristic perspective is really very different from that idea as understood by those thinking in relation to doctrines derived from 'possessive individualism' as discussed in Chapter 1. Citizenship as such is a new idea of modernity, despite reference back by those who developed it to the political ideas of classical Greece and in particular to conceptions of the proper relationship between citizen and polis. It must also always be recognized that solidaristic discussions of citizenship did borrow from another of the great trio of doctrines of modernity and allow a separation of the appropriate spheres of private existence and the public domain; it allowed for a *limited* sphere of individual possession.

In so far as 'liberal' discussions of citizenship in general now confine themselves to issues of 'rights' and 'duties', they neglect the notion of 'powers'. This is the case even when the term 'active citizen' is brought into play. The active citizen is either implicitly confined to the sphere of civil society, or explicitly directed there by those such as Green (1996) who argue from an extreme liberal (possessive individualist) position for a 'community without politics'.

Actually Marshall (1950) cannot be accused of this fault. His three levels of citizenship involved equality under the law, the necessary precondition of the negative liberties which constitute a minimalist possessive individualist basis for citizenship access to social rights, the basis of positive liberties, and the franchise which involved access to processes of political determination. There were definite obligations imposed along with this extension of political liberty and hence political power. In the Jacobin tradition the male citizen had an obligation to fight for the new world order created by the revolution. Interestingly at the high point of citizen power in the UK, in the period which led to the writing of Marshall's book, this obligation of military service was extended to women. The doctrine of Military Participation Ratio – the degree of engagement of citizens in war – is rather important in understanding citizenship in all its aspects.

In any event the aspect of solidaristic citizenship to which I want to pay most attention is that which centres on political participation. Note that there is an organicism in which this does not figure. Reactionary organicism with its doctrine of levels and places is perfectly happy with the exclusion of groups, even groups with profound obligations in terms for example of military service, from any real role in the political process. In principle, although forced to concede in practice in peacetime conditions, this was the Bismarckian approach to the regulation of the *Kaiserreich*. It is not the approach of the new, essentially Christian Democratic Germany, despite that society's disgraceful retention of an organic basis for citizenship through a *ius sanguinis*.

In Chapter 1 we noted that there is an inherent tension between the assertion of negative liberty and the existence of democracy. There is a tension, not so much in principle as in practice, or rather not in principle since the defeat of fascism, between organicism and democracy. The characteristic political form of administration in organic polities is corporatist. This survival of the conception of the role of 'estates' in the political sphere was the intellectual core of Italian and Spanish fascism and has played an important role in the development of Catholic political thinking in the twentieth century. The European Union's emphasis on 'social partners' is an essentially corporatist idea involving collaboration between the elites of labour and capital – the classic social partners, in a system mediated by the state. With the development of 'partnership' as an active device directed against social exclusion we see the invention of a third partner, 'the community', (see Geddes 1997) in which local representatives from the voluntary sector, active citizens in Green's (1996) 'Community without politics' are drawn into the corporatist process. In the UK trade unions were excluded from the corporatist bun fight by the Tories and remain excluded by a Labour Party that was originally founded expressly to represent their organizational interests. It is important to distinguish even traditional corporatism from democracy. The key differences are that under corporatism the leaders of interest groups act without any clear mechanism through which they are accountable to the constituencies they represent, and under corporatism crucial decisions are much more likely to be wholly secret.

There is no direct role for the political citizen in the corporatist framework. They are included in through membership of the group or estate to which they are considered to belong. This is of particular significance given the corporatist form of administration of land development, a process of the greatest significance for social exclusion as expressed at the local level. In reality the identification of the 'community' as an estate of the poor is, as we shall see, at best a dangerous and self-deluding myth and at worst a cynical device for facilitating their continued exclusion in terms both of their condition and from any active participation in real politics.

There is an alternative which represents the most radical end of radical Catholicism. Indeed in its liberation theology form this probably belongs in Chapter 3, but it should be introduced here. Again we are dealing with fuzzy sets. The key word is Freire's – 'empowerment'.

> *Empowerment* – For poor and dispossessed people, strength is in numbers and social change is accomplished in unity. Power is shared, not the power of a few who improve themselves at the expense of others, but the power of the many who find strength and purpose in a common vision. Liberation achieved by individuals at the expense of others is an act of oppression. Personal freedom and the development of individuals can only occur in mutuality with others.
>
> (Heaney 1995: 2)

Heaney very clearly expresses the content of Freire's key idea, which seems to me to be absolutely relevant to the discussion of 'solidaristic' conceptions of social exclusion and inclusion. In the very interesting second report of Northern Ireland's 'Democratic Dialogue' Teague and Wilson (1995) note that:

> The civil republican model of citizenship stands in sharp contrast to the liberal individualist version. In particular, it places much more emphasis on the idea of collective good and social duties and responsibilities of individuals. Thus civil republicans are strong advocates of political communities and active participation. The idea that citizenship is simply some type of legal status that confers on individuals certain rights against the state is rejected as impoverished. Individuals are regarded as only being fully enriched through social co-operation and in circumstances

where they play an active role in public life and abide by community norms and rules.

(Teague and Wilson 1995: 93)

Teague and Wilson remark that in Northern Ireland there has been a hypertrophy of what Arendt (1958) called 'communities of meaning' but that with the weakness of civil society, there is no foundation for 'communities of action', 'through which decentralised collectivists solutions are to be found to the question of order and authority' (Teague and Wilson 1995: 94). Freire's notion of empowerment is a specification both of a means of social pedagogy through which poor people transform themselves in interaction with others, and of an end, an outcome in which civil republican citizenship is expressed through communities of action. It is about outcome, but also about process. People have to be able to do it for themselves.

Plainly, organicist corporatism is not a means to this end. It is in fact deliberately designed to exclude the 'masses' from the process of decision making. Freire's ideas were put together in a Brazil dominated by economic and political elites in which the mass of the population were excluded from any role in determining the course of the social order, and in which the degree of emmiseration and social deprivation was (and remains) extreme. This system was actually highly corporatist, but with an exclusion of effective representation of both organized labour and the rural poor. In practice the introduction of a formal ideology of classical liberalism and of institutions facilitating liberal market reforms has virtually no effect on these kinds of arrangements. In Thatcher's Britain the illfares of a liberalized market were intensified by the handing over of much of urban planning from institutions which were at least in principle democratic and which were supposed to be adopting participatory processes, to exclusionary corporatist bodies in which there was a complete absence of participation in strategic decision making, the urban development corporations typified by the London Docklands Development Corporation (LDDC).

For now, we can see, I hope, that there are two versions of organicism. One, while concerned with inclusion in the sense that people are to have a place, is not concerned with emancipation. The other is absolutely about emancipation. The one is typified by the theological attitudes of Pope John Paul II. The other is characteristic of liberation theology. For the first type inclusion is about condition. For the second it must be about process. The struggle against what we now call 'exclusion' is a cultural process founded around ideas or it is nothing.

One agency which seems to be promoting a social politics based on emancipatory inclusion is the United Nations Development Programme (UNDP). There is a tension in the reports prepared under this programme between liberal and collectivist conceptions, but in association with the International Labour Organization (ILO), UNDP, especially in the former Soviet system eastern and central Europe, has argued against the liberal agendas of the IMF which have been explicitly informed by the perspectives discussed in Chapter 1 (see Deacon 1997). However, in practice the programmes of UNDP in industrialized societies have not translated into cohesive social development programmes on the ground.

There is clearly a linkage between emancipatory organicism, the perspectives both of liberation theology and of active civic republicanism, and the Marxist perspectives to be discussed in Chapter 3. Indeed Freire explicitly took the idea of dialectical development from the young Marx as the basis for his programme of social pedagogy. What these perspectives have not developed is a coherent account of the political economy of exclusion. Instead they probably rely rather too much on older Marxist versions to underpin their conceptions of appropriate social programmes. In Chapter 3 we shall examine the two available Marxist accounts of the sort of world we live in, the 'mere political economy' of regulation theory, and the emancipatory potential of autonomist thinking.

In concluding this chapter it is worth reviewing the political ideas which inform the social politics of the countries from which illustrative examples are being drawn. France is the easiest case. The overwhelming ideological foundation of the principles of French political parties from the National Front to the Communists is some version of solidarism, although of course this can be a highly exclusionary solidarism as with the National Front. Classical liberal conceptions of the nature of social politics do not have an explicit and separate political base in France but instead are represented by 'modernizing' tendencies in the mainstream parties of the right and in the socialists. In general moves towards the creation of flexibility and deregulation in France are justified by economic and market driven necessity rather than in explicit ideological terms.

Poland is a very interesting case. There is minimal popular support for economic liberalism (see Weclawowicz 1996) but the first post-communist government opted for a shock therapy move towards free markets – the Balcerowicz programme. The role of international institutions in promoting this and related agendas is considerable (see Deacon 1997). Thus in Poland we have a contradiction in that the ideological form of political life is organized around two competing versions of solidarism – post-communist and Catholic Christian democratic. However, the Catholic Church as an institution is notably absent from distributional politics (Millard 1997) and this substantially weakens the potential for the development of a social market approach to political intervention.

The UK and the USA are societies in which the neoliberal understanding of the power of globalism has triumphed in politics. This is much more complete for the institutional structures of UK politics than is the case in the US where spatial and other interests serve to mediate the practical retreat from intervention and where a real anti-globalism remains a coherent political factor. In the UK the creation of New Labour means that both political parties are committed unequivocally to servicing the logics of globalism. The Euro-sceptics are not globally sceptical. They accept the logic of global markets. It is the institutional forms of Europe which they reject. UK Prime Minister Blair's 'Christian Socialism' is neither Christian nor socialist in any meaningful sense in relation to the social politics predicated by either of these positions and particularly by their combination.

In France there are political forces to the left of socialism with considerable support and influence, and there is still a real socialist element in the Socialist Party. In the UK there is probably the potential for the emergence of such socialist forces following any development of proportional representation, although New Labour is no longer in any sense a socialist party. In the USA there has been an abandonment of politics. In Poland the enormous diversity of parties makes an account difficult, but the democratic non-former-communist left failed to pass the threshold for Sejm (parliament) entry in the 1997 election.

The most significant level for social politics is that of 'block'. The North American Free Trade Area (NAFTA) is unequivocally committed to globalization. The social politics of the European Union are in a state of tension between the logic of globalizing capital and the hegemonic lowest common denominator of solidarism shared by socialists and Christian democrats. In this politics Blair is the stalking horse of the global logic, although we must not forget that as Luttwak (1997) puts it:

> In Europe, Tony Blair is only the most blatant among today's party leaders on the Left in his disdain for poor people and other losers, his overwhelming desire to sup at the table of financial success, and his contempt for the broad mass of working stiffs with small houses, big mortgages and ugly little cars. He is certainly ill-equipped to resist the plausibilities of central bankism.
>
> (Luttwak 1997: 61)

The significance of the central bank objectives specified in the Maastricht treaty as the basis for convergence and the development of monetary union is enormous, and profoundly contradictory to any politics of solidarity. We shall return to the 'logic'/ideological position informing them in the conclusion to this book.

Exploitation matters: Marxist approaches to exclusion

The third category of the relative surplus population, the stagnant, forms a part of the active labour army, but with extremely irregular employment. Hence it furnishes to capital an inexhaustible reservoir of disposable labour-power. Its conditions of life sink below that of the average normal level of the working class; this makes it at once the broad basis of special branches of capitalist exploitation. It is characterised by a maximum of working time, and a minimum of wages . . . Its extent grows, as with the extent and energy of accumulation, the creation of the surplus population advances. But it forms at the same time a self-reproducing and self-perpetuating element of the working class, taking a proportionally greater part in the general increase of that class than the other elements.

(Marx 1977: 602)

The key Marxist concept in understanding the phenomena with which this book is concerned is that of the 'reserve army of labour', sometimes also referred to as 'the industrial reserve army'. Bauman's analysis (1987, 1997, 1998) hinges exactly on the notion that the 'socially excluded' do not constitute a reserve army of labour under the present conditions of accumulation in late capitalism:

the poor are less and less important to the reproduction of capital in their traditional role as the 'reserve army of labour'. They are no longer the object of concern for the twofold political task of recommodification of labour and limitation of working-class militancy. The previously taken-for-granted principle of social responsibility for the survival

– and, indeed, the well being – of that part of society not directly engaged by capital as producers has suddenly come under attack.

(Bauman 1987: 21)

This is a deeply Marxist analysis in form – Bauman has gone right to the heart of the matter. This is the crucial issue. The burden of this chapter will be an argument that he is wrong – that those discussed under the contemporary heading of 'social exclusion' are indeed a reserve army of labour and that we have to understand the contemporary character of capitalist restructuring as one which depends absolutely on a simultaneous development and underdevelopment of the forces of production and of the class elements which contribute to those forces of production.

Let us begin with consideration of the classical Marxist account of the 'reserve army', followed by a review of the way in which 'regulation theory', the currently fashionable (and indeed even intelligible and often sensible) version of Marxist academic theory deals with these issues. However, regulation theory remains a system centred account in which all the autonomy is yielded to capitalism and capitalists. Nelson's (1995) discussion of postindustrial capitalism, which is also considered here, is one which recognizes the significance of political action, but again see this as monopolized by capitalist interests. The discussion of 'autonomist Marxist' perspectives which concludes this chapter takes a very different view of things, at least in terms of potential.

The industrial reserve army

Marx was an assiduous reader of the Blue Books, of those extraordinarily thorough investigations conducted by Royal Commissions and House of Commons Committees which described the profoundly changing society administered by the British state during the industrial revolution. I would be very surprised indeed if he had not read the reports of the Royal Commission on the Irish Poor Law, and especially Sir George Lewis's (1836) *Report on the State of the Irish Poor in Great Britain*. Let me quote both A. Carlile in his evidence to Lewis and Lewis himself:

> The boundless coal fields beneath us and the boundless mines of labour so to speak, existing for us in Ireland, form together one of the great secrets of this part of Scotland. We are in the rare predicament of being able to obtain any required increase in our working population, without being obliged to pay the usual high penalties for creating such increased supplies viz. increased wages, loss of time and valuable commercial opportunities.
>
> (A. Carlile, quoted in Lewis 1836: 463)

the Irish have, in those branches of industry which could be easily taught either to children or adults, been a check on the combination of the English and Scotch of the Western counties, as they could be brought over almost in any numbers, at short notice, and at little expense. Thus not only can the Irish be put in place of the natives if the latter turn out, but the natives sometimes abstain from turning out, in the consciousness that their places can immediately be filled.

(Lewis 1836: 463)

Marx went to school with these students of capitalism and he learned his lesson well. The immediate function of a reserve army of labour is twofold. It exists in order to enable expansion of production without increase in unit labour costs. It exists in order to discipline employed workers through the threat of substitution. Note that Marx goes beyond this account. His reserve army is differentiated. A crucial element of it exists in order to facilitate special branches of accumulation. We shall come back to that idea in a moment.

Friend and Metcalf (1981) disliked the term 'reserve army of labour' for its economistic character and preferred to consider 'the surplus population':

> these groups include all those who are long-term unemployed; most of those for whom periods of unemployment alternate with dependence on temporary or casual part-time work; those participating in the bottom reaches of the 'black economy' outside the tax system; all those who are totally dependent on state benefits or forms of charity (including the mass of pensioners, the chronically sick and disabled, and single parent families on social security); and those people who, although in regular employment in labour-intensive sweated occupations or the state service sector, earn wages significantly below the national average and who live in households where the standard of living only exceeds the minimum poverty line because of the receipt of means tested benefits. This broad definition embraces the majority of those living in urban areas who are unemployed because they are marginal to the requirements of capital in terms of the direct production of surplus value during the current long wave of stagnation, but do not draw a hard and fast distinction between them and the low paid who are in work or those who are excluded from the workforce because of age and childcare responsibilities – because in practice this line is often crossed by individual people.

(Friend and Metcalf 1981: 119)

This account at first glance seems very similar to Marx's account of 'the stagnant element' of the 'relative surplus population' cast into contemporary language. However, there is one crucial difference. For Friend and Metcalf (1981) these categories of people are 'marginal' to the direct production of surplus value. This does allow them to contribute indirectly to the production of surplus value. It is not Bauman's (1987) account of the complete economic irrelevance of the poor. However, Marx's own account does not dismiss this group from the process of direct exploitation. On the contrary, they are the basis of special branches of such exploitation.

The crucial reason for this lies precisely in something that Friend and Metcalf (1981) recognized as significant. This is the dynamism of specific condition within the general condition of being poor. People move among the categories of benefit dependency and exploited work. Indeed the re-invention since the 1970s of 'Speenhamland' style supplementation of low wages is a system recognition of exactly this personal dynamism.[1] The only groups which might not be considered to be part of this pattern of dynamic movement to and from work are permanently disabled people and pensioners, although these categories are by no means absolutely separated from work, and especially part-time work.

There is very considerable emphasis in the literature dealing with social exclusion on 'income dynamics' i.e. movements around position in the distribution of household incomes (see Webb 1995; Goodman *et al.* 1997; Leisering and Walker 1998a). It is clearly important to understand the duration of 'the state of being excluded' and this matters profoundly for public understanding and public policy. Short term with the probability of recovery matters much less than permanent differentiation. However, of even more significance is the dynamism that Friend and Metcalf (1981) identify within the states which are associated with being poor. It is this dynamism which is the basis of the functionality of the poor as a reserve army.

Dynamism is an aspect of the capitalist social order as a system as well as of the household units nested within it.[2] The significance of the industrial reserve army lies not just in its role in disciplining labour within a given condition state of capitalism as a system, i.e. within a period when capitalism operates with a relatively stable form in terms of the social relations of production. The industrial reserve army is crucial to processes of restructuring when capitalism is in crisis.

The idea of crisis has been discussed in a seminal article by O'Connor (1981) in which he identifies the term as originating in classical Greek medicine to describe a 'turning point', a situation in which continuation in present state was not possible but in which things had to change to one or another of two possible outcomes. This is exactly analogous to the idea in chaos/complexity theory of bifurcation point. O'Connor (1981) describes capitalism as a 'crisis dependent system'. This is by no means specifically a Marxist viewpoint. Schumpeter's conception of capitalism (see Nelson 1995) as driven by waves of creative destruction is also a theory of capitalism as crisis driven, but, whereas Marxist accounts see crises as stages in the transition from capitalism to socialism and as essentially negative for capitalism as a system, for Schumpeter capitalist crises are the means by which the system develops to ever higher levels of production and general welfare achievement. We shall return to a Schumpeterian account when we consider Nelson's (1995) discussion of the development of the service sector in post-industrial capitalism.

O'Connor (1981) dismisses both the traditional 'scientific' Marxist theory of crisis as being an interruption in the accumulation of capital – accounts in which 'the subject is capital itself' (1981: 302) and neo-Marxist accounts in the radical Durkheimian tradition of critical theory in which crisis is an interruption of the normative structure of social action. It should be noted that the organicist element in the formation of the notion of social exclusion is founded in fundamentally the same sort of understanding as this latter version of crisis. O'Connor in autonomist mode argues for an understanding of crisis as involving social conflict and class struggle. His account of the role of the reserve army in relation to crisis, a role which is compatible with all Marxist accounts and indeed with Schumpeter's, is central to this understanding:

> crisis induced recreation of the reserve army of labour is a lever of accumulation to the degree that it is a level of 'capital restructuring'. This means that layoffs during the early stages of economic crises permit capital to re-establish its domination over the working class which in turn is a pre-condition for restructuring the means of production and relocating industry . . . It is not the original layoffs . . . but the 'second round unemployment' which theoretically makes the next boom possible without excessive upward pressure on wage rates. In this sense, the reserve army is the key to restructuring the means of production and also the system's capacity to enter into a new phase of expansion.
>   (O'Connor 1981: 315–16)

O'Connor is saying exactly the same thing as Paisley businessman Carlile said in 1836, although Carlile's reserve army was the latent reserve army of a dispossessed peasantry from Ireland rather than the unemployed within the capitalist industrial order itself. The significance of the latent reserve external to metropolitan capitalism but importable into it is immense. In this book the implications of this are considered in terms of consequent multi-ethnicity, but not in terms of the immigration process as such.

I want to push O'Connor's position farther than he takes it. His discussion deals with the slump–boom cycle of capitalist production. We need to consider that dynamic as a dynamic within phases of capitalism. I would argue that the recreation of a reserve army is even more important as a means towards the dynamic phase shift from one form of capitalism to another. Essentially my argument is that the reserve army is a crucial means to the restructuring of the capitalist social order as a whole: it is the means within a Schumpeterian account whereby the countervailing power of labour is overcome and the forces which drive change, including new technologies and new forms of managerial control, are given the sway they need.

Auyero (1997) has reintroduced a development of the classical Marxist conception of the reserve army which derives from Latin American development sociology of the 1970s. He has reminded (or informed) us that:

> The structural historicist perspective on marginality . . . understood that the functioning of what they called 'the dependent labour market' was generating an excessive amount of unemployment. This 'surplus population' transcends the logic of the Marxian concept of the 'industrial

reserve army' and led the authors to coin the term 'marginal mass'. The 'marginal mass' was neither superfluous nor useless; it was marginal because it had been rejected by the society that created it.

(Auyero 1997: 508–9)

This term and the conception it embodies is extremely valuable because Auyero (1997) is picking up the spatial segregation element and linking it to the role of the 'excluded' in the general logic of the development of capitalist production through underdevelopment. The 'bringing back home of underdevelopment' is a crucial aspect of the autonomist account although we shall find subsequently that marginalization is not the strategy by which post-industrial capitalism is seeking to achieve underdevelopment in its metropolitan core. Instead the poor are managed through two strategies. Most are integrated into a pattern of formal work at low wages alternating with dependency on benefits. Some are controlled through incarceration. Let us turn from O'Connor's (1981) account of the means of restructuring to the most general account of the nature of the outcome of that restructuring: regulation theory.

Regulation theory: transition codified – post-industrial capitalism: the means specified

In his review of *Post-Fordism* Amin (1994) identifies three theoretical positions, namely the regulation approach, the flexible specialization approach and the neo-Schumpeterian approach. All are concerned with qualitative change, although the middle perspective, flexible specialization, is really rather limited and confined to a consideration of the organization of production alone. I want to concentrate here on 'regulation theory' described by Amin as the product of an intellectual current which wanted to develop:

a theoretical framework which could encapsulate and explain the paradox within capitalism between its inherent tendency towards instability, crisis and change, and its ability to coalesce and stabilise around a set of institutions, rules and norms which serve to secure a relatively long period of economic stability.

(Amin 1994: 7)

However, it is not stability but change which preoccupies contemporary regulation theory. They posit, as Esser and Hirsch (1994: 73) put it: 'a nonlinear theory of capitalist development'. The regulation theory school at its most general distinguishes between 'the regime of accumulation', that is the general pattern of organization of the processes of capitalist production towards the end of accumulation, and 'the mode of regulation' which describes the complex of institutions and normative structures which surround and govern the processes of capitalist reproduction. The combined effect of change in both mode of accumulation and mode of regulation is a transition to a new form of capitalism.

In most of the discussion of post-Fordism the regime of accumulation is privileged. There is continual discussion of, for example, the changes from mass production to flexible specialization. However, the regulation theory account is not one of changes in reproduction predicated on changes in production, or at least it is not such an account in principle. In other words we should not think of the regime of accumulation as 'determining' the mode of regulation. Both change together, in interaction.

Although the concept of 'mode of societalization' is usually considered as an element in a fivefold extension of the original duo, it seems to me to be better considered as a specification of a crucial aspect of the 'mode of regulation'. Amin (1994: 8) describes this concept as referring to: 'a series of political compromises, social alliances and hegemonic processes of domination which feed into a pattern of mass integration and social cohesion, thus serving to underwrite and stabilise a given development push.' The Keynes/ Beveridge Welfare State coupled with the rights of trade unions to effective organization can be considered to represent a crucial compromise between organized labour and capital. In particular it channelled accumulation away from absolute surplus value expropriation which depended on the exploitative emmiseration of workers and towards relative surplus value expropriation which involves the use of technology and labour process organization to increase the volume productivity of workers. This latter was the essence of Fordism. It was the basis of a general raising of all metropolitan sector incomes during the Fordist era. The owners got more absolutely but wages still rose. This applied both to direct wages and to components of the social wage in the form of welfare services in kind.

The move away from a welfare system which facilitated this process has been described (although not described in terms of the absolute/relative surplus value expropriation concept) by Jessop (1994) as involving the development of a Schumpeterian workfare state, 'governed by the aim "to promote product, process and market innovation in open economies" (hence Schumpeterian) and "to subordinate social policy to the needs of labour market flexibility and/or the constraints of international competition" (hence workfare)' (Amin 1994: 27–8).[3] Jessop himself remarks that:

> post-Fordist growth need not generalise core workers' rising incomes to other workers and/or the economically inactive [as Fordism had – DSB]. Indeed, as post-Fordist accumulation will be more oriented to world-wide demand, global competition could further limit the scope for general prosperity and encourage market-led polarization of incomes.
>
> (Jessop 1994: 254)

Graham (1992) has argued that regulation theory constitutes a discourse which pretends to be a science and that it needs to be challenged in epistemological terms. While agreeing with the detail of her criticism, I disagree with its foundation. Regulation theory, despite the best efforts of those associated with it, remains an account of system rather than of action. A postmodernist critique of it remains merely epistemological, merely concerned with the issue of its validity as the foundation of a claim to knowledge. All Graham can offer as an alternative is a general endorsement of the validity of competing discourses with different social group foundations. A realist perspective enables us to accept that capitalism does exist and that the kinds of things described by regulation theory may indeed be real, but they are neither permanent nor changeable only at the systemic level. Graham (1992), as a postmodernist, will not grasp the ontological nettle of active social constructionism, expressed rather well in Karl Marx's Thesis XI on Feuerbach: 'The Philosophers have described the world: the point however is to change it.'

Regulation theory in the hands of Jessop (1994) and many others is a distinctly sad song with little potential for stirring up social action for change. Even Lipietz (1994), who makes a genuine effort at constructing a politics, is left with little more than palliation. In the language of autonomist Marxism, this is Marxist analysis as 'mere political economy' and 'for Capitalism'. Certainly regulation theory underpins the continuing wailing of 'globalization is inevitable and capitalism has won' which is the fundamental political economy of the 'New Centre Politics of Flexibility', represented in the late twentieth century by US President Bill Clinton and UK Prime Minister Tony Blair.

Two writers from the general regulation theory position who are by no means so pessimistic are Peck and Tickell (1994). Their arguments potentially resemble the historical analysis of early capitalism suggested by Inglis (1972) to the effect that at points of change there are alternatives and that what happens is a product of willed action – things can be different. However, Peck and Tickell (1994) do not quite bring it this far, emphasizing instead the instability of the present situation and of the neoliberal programme for resolving its difficulties. Of particular significance is the 'tendency to social polarisation with the attendant possibility of either disruptive collective action or social breakdown' (Peck and Tickell 1994: 294).

The problem with regulation theory is that it has no prescriptions to make other than moral ones. Lee's (1995) interesting article argues for the 'exogeneity of the social reproduction of labour' (1995: 1577), that is the relative independence of the forms of the social reproduction of labour from determination by the specific forms of capitalist production and re-production of commodities in general. This means that under capitalist social relations we can develop 'circuits of power independently of the circuit of capital' (Lee 1995: 1593) and on the basis of these establish a different moral economy in the social sphere. This is really a kind of political economy version of the line expressed by Bauman. It seems to me that Lee has slipped from exploitation to domination as the central relation of capitalism itself. This is a very general shift in social analysis but it is perhaps surprising to find it coming from a writer with such a political economy style. Regulation theory is full of interesting ideas but at the end is a deeply gloomy and disempowering account of potential for change because of the systemic power it gives to capital organization.

Nelson's (1995) account of the development of 'post-industrial' capitalism seems to have been written in isolation from the literature on post-Fordism which he does not reference. There is much in common between the accounts, although Nelson's is the better, precisely because he identifies the role of managerial agency expressed in production, marketing and politics, in the reformation of the social context. Nelson's account is essentially, and explicitly, Schumpeterian, in that he produces a description of a social order of which he thoroughly disapproves, but which he does not see as being in any sort of crisis at all. The implications for our considerations are summarized thus:

> post-industrial capitalism does not involve any shift in the fundamental processes of capitalism, as reflected in the competitive search for economic advantage or political dominance . . . What his new and blended form of capitalism does, however, is produce a transformation, a qualitative and discontinuous shift in class structure. That is, the contrast of past and present is indicated not merely by the blended form capitalism assumes but also by its influences on inequality. In a previous time, economic development fed social development by diminishing inequality; today economic development escalates inequality.
>
> (Nelson 1995: 14)

Nelson attacks the 'Latin American' analogy exemplified by Therborn's (1985) thesis of the 'Brazilianization of advanced capitalism' which argues that advanced capitalism is likely to develop a tripartheid system of division among an excluded poor, an insecure middle mass, and an exploitative rich, but he is not attacking the account of polarized inequality it represents. Rather he sees not a disjointed economy with a marginalized poor, but rather 'a functionally integrated economy with a top and a bottom both part of the same fabric, the same overall master trend toward escalating rationalisation in business' (Nelson 1995: 39). In this respect the evidence supports his account for the United States and it is clear that the development of workfare as an integrative mechanism is intended to have the same effect in the UK.

This account is a complete refutation of Bauman's (1997) notion that the new poor are an economically irrelevant surplus population who are not even required as a source of consumption:

> The prospect of solidarity with the poor and desolate may be further, and decisively, undermined by the fact that, for the first time in human history, the poor so to speak have lost their social uses. They are not the vehicle of personal repentance and salvation; they are not the hewers of wood and drawers of water, who feed and defend; they are not the 'reserve army of labour', nor the flesh and bones of military power either; and most certainly they are not the consumers who will provide the effective 'market clearing' demand and start up recovery. The new poor are fully and truly useless and redundant, and thus become burdensome 'others' who have outstayed their welcome.
>
> (Bauman 1997: 4–5)

Far from it – in the new sectors through which consumption is delivered by large-scale private capital – and here we must pause to note the almost complete neglect in 'consumptionist' sociology of any consideration of the actual production of that consumption through the capitalist organization of delivering labour: 'What is new (and news) about the working poor is their connection to corporate growth – to industries in the core sector rather than in the margins of a peripheral undermodernised economy' (Nelson 1995: 54).

Nelson's account of the organization of the new low-waged service sector in the USA with a division between highly skilled and credentialized management and a low wage insecure workforce, is convincing and significant. It represents a real political economy of 'poor work' and places the generation of profits from the exploitation of those who are forced to do 'poor work' (Welfare to Work after the Chancellor of the Exchequer Gordon Brown) as central to the development of advanced capitalism as a whole. However, Nelson, as a Schumpeterian, is profoundly pessimistic about the development of any kind of counter to these changes. This concerns and worries him but he concludes that what we are experiencing is 'inequality without class conflict'.

Let us turn to an account which understands the potential of class action as the determinant of which sort of future we shall actually have.

Social proletarians: underdevelopment as exclusion

A central proposition of the autonomist position is the notion of 'the social factory', the arena of the reproduction of labour power in a capitalist system as well as of the production of commodities in that system. Cleaver (1979) explained it thus:

> [Mario Tronti] focuses on how the analysis of circulation and reproduction in Volume II of *Capital* also involved the reproduction of classes. This insight meant that the equation of capital with the 'factory', characteristic of Marxist political economy, was clearly inadequate. The reproduction of the working class involves not only work in the factory but also work in the home and in the community of homes. This realization brought into sharp focus the importance of Marx's long discussion of the reserve army in Volume I's chapters on accumulation. Accumulation means accumulation of the reserve army as well as the active army, of those who work at reproducing the class as well as those who produced other commodities (besides labour power). The 'factory' where the working class worked was the society as a whole, a social factory.
>
> (Cleaver 1979: 57)

This extensive definition of the 'factory' matters because from an autonomist perspective the contradictions in a capitalist system do not stem from abstract aspects of the logic of the system as such, the classical mechanist Marxist position, but instead are represented by the working class as the active contradiction which in denying exploitation, denies the validity of capitalism as a system in general. From this perspective crises and trans- formations are points at which, to use the Gramscian terminology, the war of position characteristic of 'stable' periods within capitalism, is replaced by a war of movement in which the terms of engagement between capitalism on the one hand and the working class on the other are redefined.

This account actually corresponds perfectly well with 'capitalism's' Marxism as expressed by those who endorse globalization; capitalism has liberated itself in space through the use of global repositioning of both money and plant, and at the point of production trade union power has been so reduced that managers have had restored to them 'the right to manage', i.e. the right to direct the trajectory of production against any competing vision of how it should be. The new 'hybrid' forms of service delivering capital- ism (Nelson 1995) represent an innovative development based on reflexive expertise of managers, in the domination of workers, which actually seems to have led to the renewed significance of absolute emmiserating surplus value expropriation.

The significance of the idea of the 'social factory' is that conflicts between capital and labour occur not only at the point of production, but around all aspects of reproduction as well. Capitalism and capitalists seek to control not only the making of commodities in general, but also the terms and conditions under which labour power is reproduced in particular. This cannot be left 'exogenous' from the relations of production in general. The political implication of this analysis is that no privilege attaches to class action at the point of production, to, in the Italian autonomist's expression, 'the politics of Fiat'. All struggles over both production and reproduction matter.

In the contemporary war of movement (I agree with Peck and Tickell that we have not yet settled into a condition describable as a war of position) capital is certainly still on the broad offensive. Negri (1988) has remarked that:

> capital's science of domination was far ahead of us. At the time when we were introducing the concept of the mass worker, and, by implica- tion, a critique of the category of 'labour-power' in favour of a concept of the dynamism of the working class, capital, for its part, had already made tremendous advances in its own practice, as regards the theory of domination and redressing the balance of power . . . For, while from a working-class viewpoint the revolutionary practice of the mass worker was being advanced within individual factories, and within the overall inter-locked system of factories and companies, capital was already responding in overall, global and social terms – in terms of global domination and control.
>
> (Negri 1988: 206–7)

The implication of this, correct, account is that the redefinition of the future is for the moment in capital's hands.[4]

The central autonomist idea which relates specifically to social exclusion is that of underdevelopment. Let me quote again from Cleaver (1977):

> development and underdevelopment are understood here neither as the outcome of historical processes (as bourgeois economists recount) nor as the processes themselves (as many Marxists use the term). They are rather two different *strategies* by which capital seeks to control the working class . . . they are always co-existent because hierarchy is the key to capital's control and development is always accompanied by relative or absolute underdevelopment for others in order to maintain that hierarchy . . . By development I mean a strategy in which working class income is raised in exchange for more work . . . The alternative strategy, in which income is reduced in order to impose the availability for work, I call a strategy for underdevelopment.
>
> (Cleaver 1977: 94, original emphasis)

Underdevelopment seems to me to be a good term to use as a synonym for the actual processes that constitute social exclusion. The socially excluded are those parts of the population who have been actively underdeveloped. This kind of formulation is particularly appropriate in that it breaks down what seem to be increasingly less meaningful distinctions between nations in the global system, or at least between those elements in almost all nations who relate to industrial capitalism directly rather than as non-proletarian producers of commodities for it. Peasants may be a different story but for everybody else the relations of the industrial system hold.

Therborn's (1985) thesis of the 'Brazilianization of advanced capitalism' is a thesis of underdevelopment. The interesting use of the idea of a 'fourth world' as employed by Harrison (1982) to describe places within the localities of advanced metropolitan capitalism in general, and in particular within the world city of London, is likewise an underdevelopment account. Harrison uses this term to describe neighbourhoods within which social conditions are so relatively disadvantaged that despite being only three or four miles from Hampstead, one of London's most affluent areas, they have more in common in terms of conditions of life with 'third world' slums. We may follow Nelson and agree that post-industrial capitalism is not really characterized by the economic marginalization which is the basis of such experiences in the (traditionally understood) third world, but the actual content of experiences is remarkably similar.

The crucial point about the thesis of underdevelopment is that it is a thesis of exploitation and a thesis of emmiseration. Paul Sweezy has made the point, in his foreword to Braverman's *Labor and Monopoly Capital*, that:

> Marx's General Law of Capital Accumulation, according to which the advance of capitalism is characterised by the amassing of wealth at one pole and of deprivation and misery at the other . . . far from being the

egregious fallacy which bourgeois social science has long held it to be, has in fact turned out to be one of the best founded of all Marx's insights into the capitalist system.

(Sweezy in Braverman 1974: xii)

The 'social proletariat', the 'stagnant reserve army of labour', are not irrelevant to the accumulation logic of contemporary capitalism. On the contrary, their existence is absolutely crucial to it. They matter because they are necessary as a means to bringing the new social order into existence. They matter because the exploitation of them is crucial to the continued accumulation process in the new form of capitalism which is being created. No capitalism of a post-Fordist/post-industrial general form can do without them. The account of underdevelopment suggests that social exclusion is not an accidental by-product of capitalist development but absolutely intrinsic to it. Thus when Silver (1994) correctly considers that

there are differences of opinion within the [regulation] school as to the likely course of global capitalism since the crisis. It is not clear whether the emerging regime will pursue high quality employment in a post-Fordist regime of flexible regulation or revert to a competitive strategy of externalizing market uncertainties through low-quality, low-wage jobs subject to numerical flexibility.

(Silver 1994: 551)

the crucial point is that it will do both at the same time and in the same places.

I regard the autonomist account as profoundly optimistic and hopeful. This may seem somewhat strange since it identifies 'social exclusion', if that term is interpreted as I argue it should be as a synonym for 'underdevelopment', as an essential characteristic of the dynamic transformation of contemporary capitalism *and* as a necessary characteristic of the form of capitalism which capitalists want. I have deliberately used the class rather than system label here. The point is that the system has potentials, attractor states to use the vocabulary of complexity, but which of them actually comes into being is a matter for class action. Capitalists are functioning as class warriors. They are certainly on the advance but they won't necessarily win. It can be done differently.

The social proletariat, the excluded, are not passive observers in all of this. They are certainly not, as Cleaver (1977: 86) puts it, 'spectators at the global waltz of capitalism'. On the contrary their self-activity, their autonomous self-organization, is crucial to the struggle about which kind of social order can be brought into being.

The account being presented here is an account which emphasizes people's role as producers. Those like Bauman (1998), who are putting a post-modernist gloss on Marxism, have followed critical theory's obsession with people not as producers but as consumers, and have thereby interpreted the 'excluded' as largely irrelevant to processes of consumption under capitalism.

In fact the poor of advanced industrial societies do consume and there are so many of them to do so. There are even differentiated forms of consumption for them in cheap supermarkets targeted at these groups. Capitalism dismisses no prospective consumers.[5] However, the thesis being expressed here is that production remains central and that it is as producers that we can best understand the poor.

Conclusion

Unesco (United Nations Educational, Scientific and Cultural Organization) established the MOST programme in 1992. MOST stands for the Management of Social Transformations. The second policy paper produced by MOST deals with social exclusion on a world scale. At first the participants in the symposium on which it reports seem to be agreeing with Bauman (1998):

> The concept of exclusion has come into ever greater use with the deepening of the social crisis. Contrary to what occurred in the Industrial Revolution of the last century, the rich now have less and less need for the labour power of the poor. Exclusion seems to have replaced exploitation as the primary cause of poverty.
>
> (Bessis 1995: 13)

However, they immediately qualify this position:

> The two phenomena of exploitation and exclusion are not, however, totally independent of one another. Can one say, as does Philippe Van Parijs that the successes obtained by European welfare states and trade unions in the struggle against exploitation rendered exclusion the predominant form of social injustice? . . . These questions regarding the respective importance of the two phenomena are not a matter of simple quarrel among specialists. The response one gives to them generates policies that assign priority either to the struggle against exploitation or the battle against exclusion.
>
> (Bessis 1995: 13)

The argument being presented here is that exclusion is a crucial contemporary form of exploitation, and that indeed there is nothing new about it. It has a great deal in common with the form of exploitation that characterized the beginning of the Industrial Revolution itself. Hence the renewed utility of the ideology of that period, expressed with a deal less honest and clarity than it was by Ricardo and Nassau Senior, but expressed in essentially the same terms (see Inglis 1972). The battle against exclusion must be a battle against exploitation.

Of course the above argument requires not only analytical assertion but also empirical demonstration. That is the purpose of Chapter 5 in which particular attention is paid to the nature and scale of contemporary processes of exploitation through an examination of the distribution of income and the sources of that distribution. The focus of attention here is on the contemporary complex of poor work and full or partial benefit dependency that constitutes the attractor state for the poor in this transition phase.

It is important that the statement that exclusion is exploitation is also a statement about what exclusion is not. Exclusion is not domination. It is not to do with identity considered either as something either intrinsic or self-chosen. It is to do with specific economic relations. This is a highly contentious point. Let me say straight away that I actually do think that a neo-Durkheimian treatment of exclusion in relation to identity is worthwhile and that exclusion can really be thought to have a lot to do with excluded identities, but that is not what the current debate on social exclusion is essentially concerned with. In other words 'identity exclusion' although always subject to modification by the economic relations of phases of capitalism, has an intrinsic content of its own and may exist under all forms of economic relation.

And yet I wonder if identity and the domination of specific identities constructed around gender, race/ethnicity, sexual orientation, age and being disabled (that proper active notion is so close to being excluded), ever really exist *sui generis*? In examining the contemporary expression of inequality in relation to these 'identities of condition', we shall find that class situation always modifies their expression. In the language of chaos/complexity, there is no simple superposition. All interact with class so that we can, for example, never understand the consequences of gender without understanding it in relation to class. Of course this statement should be reversible and it is. If there is interaction we can never understand class without considering gender. The prioritizing of class which is central to this book's account of social exclusion depends on the active relation between class and capitalism, on the links among the nested systems and the way in which collective action on class can modify and even transform the character of the system which contains it, but which it contradicts.

Put simply I cannot understand domination without an economic dimension. Bourdieu (1990) using a very different language came to a rather similar position when he recognized the ever present significance of the politico-economic field. There is a tendency in contemporary social theory to write class relations out all together, to such an extent that some postmodernists are having to say rather shamefacedly that it too is a domain of identity. This involves a kind of reversion to what Meiksins Wood (1986) described as the position of the New True Socialists

The New True Socialists all have one premise in common: the working class has no privileged position in the struggle for socialism in that class situation does not give rise to socialist politics any more naturally than does any other.

(Meiksins Wood 1986: 6)

although in the contemporary academy the notion of any sort of struggle for socialism has tended to be replaced by much more generalized notion of emancipation, exactly from domination. The equation of exclusion with exploitation presented in this chapter will inform all the rest of the analysis in this book. Following those who developed the ideas of autonomist Marxism, C.L.R. James (1986 [1950]) and Raya Dunayevska, Johnson and Forrest, the autonomy of struggle for what postmodernists call identity groups, will always be recognized and asserted. There are no lead elements in the social proletariat in the social factory which is society as a whole. However, it is class relation which counts, however distinctive identity makes that relation, and with the distinctiveness of that relation always recognized. We have a universal project here.

PART TWO

Dynamic society – dynamic lives

This chapter links the conceptual discussions reviewed in Part 1 with the empirical material which is examined in Chapters 5 and 6. It does so by reviewing three strands of dynamic thinking in contemporary social science in terms of their implications for the phenomenon and processes of 'social exclusion'. The first is the idea that there has been some sort of categorical transformation in the nature of the capitalist social order since the mid-1960s. This is usually described as a shift from a Fordist to a post-Fordist social order. The general character of the post-Fordist thesis was reviewed in Chapter 3. We return to it here to identify its, usually implicit, essentially dynamic character. The next strand to be considered is the developing empirical dynamism typified by the collection edited by Leisering and Walker (1998a). This approach is possible because of the development of longitudinal studies charting the trajectories of individuals and households through long periods of time. Although such studies are necessarily micro in character, the accounts generated by them, even when these have gone no further towards the macro than mere aggregation of individual case data (as is the case for income distribution studies), have forced us to recognize the dynamism of the social. This is a very clear illustration of the realist premise that we know the world because it makes itself known to us as we develop the tools for knowing it – here the macroscopic instrumentation of computing based data management. The last strand to be considered here will be the potential contribution of the conceptual vocabulary of complexity/chaos theory not only for understanding the dynamics of the social order and of individual biographies taken separately, but also as a way of integrating our understanding of macro and micro trajectories through employing the idea of reflexively interacting nested systems.

Let us now turn to a consideration of the nature of the change in social order which is the context of any sensible discussion of social exclusion as process and condition.

Post-industrial, postmodern, post-socialist? Advanced industrial societies towards the year 2000

Therborn's proposition of the 'Brazilianization of advanced capitalism' (1985: 32–3) is a good starting point for a consideration of the transformation which seems to be going on in the economic base of advanced capitalism in the late 1990s. Therborn considers that we are seeing a tripartheid division of the social system into one headed by a super, and super-exploitative, rich with a 'squeezed middle' of relatively but not absolutely secure workers and a large and emmiserated poor.

Much of this book is concerned with an elaboration and very considerable qualification of this theme, but the idea is an important one even if reduced to its most basic element. That is to say it indicates that something is changing. It is fashionable in social science to use the prefix 'post' to describe the contemporary social world. There are a variety of 'posts', of 'afters': postmodern, post-industrial, post-Fordist – three favourites with different focuses and emphases but all implying that something has changed. Let us take them in order of declining simplicity. The term 'post-industrial' is relatively straightforward at first sight. It is used, in the simple sense, to describe an important transformation of the sort of work done by people for wages in advanced industrial countries. The whole point of the description 'advanced industrial' is that the production systems of such societies are/were (this clumsy formation is meant to indicate that things have changed but not in a uniform way) characterized by the production and primary distribution of physical commodities by wage labour working under a factory system. Most of industrial employment is in the form of manufacturing of goods, but there are important related areas which do not involve direct manufacturing, notably mining, construction and the 'blue collar' services of goods transport, the production and distribution of gas, electricity and water, and the manual component of information communication by post and telecommunications. Non-industrial employment includes agricultural production, secondary distribution through retail processes, and a range of private and public service employment including financial services and the components of welfare state activities. The industrial revolution was precisely the process of the generalization of the production of commodities by factory-based industrial systems.

Relatively recently the continuous growth in both the absolute numbers of industrial workers and the proportion of all adults who fit into this category has gone into sudden and steep reverse in precisely the countries which have had the longest tradition of this process of development. It is important to recognize that this is a recent trend. Even in the UK where this process began rather early, the 51-year-old author entered an industrial world of work as a young adult. In terms of the numbers and proportion of all adults engaged in industrial work, the UK peaked as recently as the early 1960s and the peaks for European countries and the USA were even later (see respectively Martin and Rowthorn 1986; Bluestone and Harrison 1982).

It is also important to note that so far as the global system is concerned, the processes of both absolute and relative industrialization are proceeding apace. Of course we must remember that the decline in employment in industry is far greater than the decline in the productive output of industry. In most countries other than the UK decline in employment has been associated with actual large scale growth in industrial output. Even in the UK there has been a good deal of jobless (and sometimes job destroying) growth.

Deindustrialization has multiple causes. At the systemic level an important factor has been a general massive growth in labour productivity as a consequence of the combination of technological innovation and the development of new production management techniques. On a global scale there has been the development of a 'new international division of labour' with the creation of industrial systems in previously peasant societies, much of which has been fuelled by the export of capital by transnationals from the original core zones of industrial capitalism. The collapse of the 'second' world of soviet-style systems has opened up both the possibilities for such investment (especially in China) and brought into competition cheap producers of basic industrial staples, although it has also caused deindustrialization with the collapse of the eastern European military-industrial complex.

In the UK in particular there has been an explicit national factor in that public policy through the maintenance of a high exchange rate in the early 1980s and through a variety of meso-economic planning and development mechanisms, has privileged finance capital and the 'city' over manufacturing capital. In effect the revenues of North Sea oil have contributed to the destruction of the UK's manufacturing system – the economic consequences of Mrs Thatcher and the policies of her chancellors,[1] which were both economic and concerned with the relative advantage of one section of capital, and explicitly political and intended to destroy the capacity of the organized trade union movement in its citadels of power.

The term 'post-Fordist' originates with the French regulation theory school (see Amin 1994) which was discussed in Chapter 3. Whereas deindustrialization leading to a 'post-industrial' social order is an evident process with the idea of 'post-industrial' representing a transformation of quantity into quality, the change from Fordist to post-Fordist is inherently qualitative. The term 'Fordist' describes a mode of production organized around techniques of mass production and geared to systems of mass consumption. The macroeconomic management of this system is geared towards maintaining employment in order to maximize the potential of wage based demand as a basis for consumption. It is Keynesian both at the national level and in relation to the management of international economic relations through the institutions created for that purpose by Keynes himself. An important component of this process of regulation is the provision of universalist social welfare and particularly of insurance based wage substitution benefits – the Beveridge element in the whole scheme. Post-Fordist production is a product of technological innovations and new management practices which permit 'flexible specialization' through batch production as opposed to the massive homogeneous runs of the Fordist era. Such flexible specialization requires a flexible labour market and is associated with the differentiation of labour and of its rewards.

Two important characteristics of the Fordist/Keynesian social order were the shape of its income distribution and the pattern of available social mobility. Lipietz (1998), one of the key theorists of post-Fordism, has described the change from the 'Montgolfier' society in which most people and households were in the middle – the shape of a hot air balloon – to an hourglass society with what US commentators call 'the squeezed middle'. He remarks that in 'the homelands of flexibilization' (the USA and UK) increasing inequality is the product of three broad tendencies, namely a shift in factor share of incomes from wages to property, a cut in cash welfare transfers to households and increasing disparities in earned incomes (Lipietz 1998: 180). Although the argument is probably wrong about the nature of work in post-industrial capitalism, Lipietz's remark that 'If under Fordism, one could argue that "the rich lived off the expenditure of the poor", i.e. wage workers' expenditure accounted for the turnover of entrepreneurs, in the case of the hourglass society "the poor live off what trickles down from the expenditure of the rich"' (1998: 182) is indicative of the character of change.

The other structural change which matters in this transition, indeed is fundamental to any dynamic discussion at the level of individuals and households, is the change in the possibility of social mobility. Leisering and Walker (1998b) point out that

> Individual mobility is crucial to modernity. It is a functional prerequisite of change in social structures . . . Mobility is also a powerful means by which people drive forward their ambitions in life. Irrespective of the actual mobility that occurs, the idea of mobility is fundamental to the legitimization of Western Societies. The promise of mobility allows 'open societies' to maintain a system of firmly established structural inequalities. The optimism about macro-dynamics, the belief in societal progress, translates at the micro-level into the belief in individual progress.
>
> (Leisering and Walker 1998b: 4–5)

There is important evidence that the shift from industrial to post-industrial social structures involves a closure of mobility opportunities. Erikson and Goldthorpe (1992) have noted that the history of mobility patterns may well involve changes of kind, the crossing of thresholds in which periods with relatively high levels of mobility are succeeded by periods in which mobility is much more constrained. This idea of 'developmental threshold' is very similar to the idea of phase shift and we shall return to it in the discussion of complex dynamics which concludes this chapter. Certainly there is evidence that mobility is closing down in post-industrial societies. Such closure is central to any consideration of social exclusion and it is particularly significant that spatial location may be a determinant factor in it.

Whereas deindustrialization is a descriptive term and post-Fordism is an idea from political economy, the notion of postmodernity has multiple roots in considerations of cultural form and reflection on the nature of ideas themselves. Here the 'after' is after modernity, after an era characterized by the general belief in the use of reason as the foundation of social progress. Therborn (1995) has defined modernity 'as an epoch *tuned to the future*, conceived here as likely to be different from and positively better than the present and the past' (1995: 4, original emphasis). Postmodernism is a powerful intellectual school which seeks to deprivilege 'grand narratives' and emphasize differentiation in knowledge and in social practices. It is virtually universal in the academy, has some significance in cultural debates, and plays only the role of background (but not wholly insignificant) noise in social politics where the important debates are between liberal and collectivist interpretations of political economy.

The reality of deindustrialization is accepted by all. The idea of a transition from a Fordist to post-Fordist era is quite broadly considered appropriate. The idea that our era is postmodern is seriously disputed by those who like King (1996) argue that we live in a period of late modernity which is certainly different from that which existed through the mid-period of the twentieth century but which remains profoundly affected by its basis in capitalism and by the role of arguments about the use of the results of 'reason' in the conduct of politics. Sayer (1995) notes pertinently that while the academy debates postmodernity, that oldest of modern conceptual sets, liberal political economy, is more important as a basis for political ideology and process than it has been for more than a century. It may be that the modernist idea of soviet style progress is fragmented and dissolved but capitalism's version of modernist theory is alive and well and kicking very hard. Much of this book is about who is being kicked and how.

Nelson (1995) has employed the term 'post-industrial' in a more analytic way than the simple descriptive usage which it has had in preceding discussion. His arguments, founded in a consideration of development in the United States, are important and convincing. He puts it like this:

> My argument looks not to any crisis in capitalism but to a new vigor and resources – to the Schumpeterian concept of creative energy – that *activates* the corporate quest for profits . . . The centrepiece of my position is that in recent years corporations have acquired new resources, qualitatively different from those available in the past. These resources are organisational and knowledge based and are tantamount to a revolution in the inventory of tactics and strategies available to corporations . . . corporations have used these strategies to intensify competition, affect greater political control, and widen the gap between rich and poor in America today.
>
> (Nelson 1995: 20, original emphasis)

This account of reflexive agency in all of the spheres of the organization of production, of delivering consumption, and of politics itself, is extremely important.

The ideas which surround the description of 'post-industrial' and the analytical frame represented by 'post-Fordist' are essentially complementary. However, even taken together, the descriptive accounts at best begin to deal with the implications of change for the lives of people and for the ways in which they act, both individually and collectively. 'Postmodernity' as a project is one of disaggregation and separation, and whatever the limitations of the idea set, its very existence is indicative of a change in relation to social action. Nelson's careful analytical account of 'post-industrial capitalism' brings explicit agency back in, agency against equality. There are two key determinist statements in the Marxist canon. One is that 'base determines superstructure' and regulation theory is essentially a sophisticated gloss on that proposition. The other is that 'social being determines consciousness'. It is worth thinking about that as a way of understanding the relationship between social change and social exclusion because consciousness is the basis of action. The exploitative rich certainly act in their own interests. The interesting question is whether the rest of us will act in ours.

There are basically two models for advanced industrial societies. One is represented by the USA where a holding constant of the absolute value of wages has led to a relative emmiseration of blue collar and routine white collar employees associated with the development of a highly profitable new sphere of low waged services, but a maintenance of overall employment levels. The fundamental basis of this is low wages. Note that low wages can be maintained in a system with relatively low levels of unemployment only if legislation is used to destroy the organizational capacity of workers. In the USA this is a function of civil suit. In the UK it has involved both the criminalizing of picketing and the outlawing of sympathetic action. Union busting is very important. The other type of system is the developed European norm of France and Germany where institutional arrangements have preserved relativities in real wages and there are high levels of wage substitution benefits, but there is also a high level of unemployment, particularly among labour market entrants. It should be noted that this style is now under considerable ideological and political attack. In Poland structural readjustment has been uneven and localized in its effects by region with very high levels of unemployment among displaced peasant workers and women in particular places and sectors but job retention in others based on trade union power. The UK manages to replicate the worst elements of the European and US systems with high levels of unemployment associated with the development of low waged service and manufacturing sectors.

The UK Liberal Democrat-initiated Commission on Wealth Creation and Social Cohesion described the situation thus:

> One side-effect of the new economic era is that a sizeable minority see their incomes rise and also enjoy a fair amount of security, but the

majority have to struggle to keep incomes stable, and many experience declining incomes along with greater insecurity. More importantly, people no longer live in the same universe of opportunity; there are winners and losers, and the gains of the winners do not trickle down to the losers. Widening income differentials result in a serious disjunction in the commitment of different groups to the values and institutions of society.

(Dahrendorf 1995: 15)

The report of this commission is succinct and clear, in marked contrast to the report of the Labour-initiated Commission on Social Justice (Borrie 1994) and its identification of the social consequences of economic change is correct in terms of broad tendencies. However, as always, the devil is in the details, and it is in the details that the Liberal Democrat initiative got it wrong, in a most revealing and significant way. The Commission asserted that:

Exclusion is the greatest risk accompanying the opportunities of the new economic era. Significant numbers of people lose their hold on the labour market, then on the social and political participation in their community. An underclass emerges, consisting of people who live their separate lives often characterised by a combination of destitution, dependence on welfare payments and other benefits, occasional wind-falls, petty or not so petty crime, and apathy. The underclass may not be a new phenomenon.

(Dahrendorf 1995: 15)

What is absolutely missing from that story is the significance of the com-bination of low wages, insecure employment, and dependence on means tested benefit supplements to low incomes. In other words the account is one of separation from work, not obligation to engage in poor work. Poor work is the big story. Moreover, contrary to one possible reading of the passage quoted, 'the underclass', or rather the complicated ensemble of personal trajectories which constitute the emergent phenomenon to which that term is applied, is a reappearing phenomenon, not something we have always had with us. It is a phenomenon of the reorganization of the social and political order in the interests of some and against the interests of others, of a restoration of the social relations of the pre-Keynesian era. Social exclusion is an active process. Insecurity and low wages are the basis for a reconstruction of the relationship between labour and capital on a global scale. Things have changed (been changed) for the worse but they can be changed again for the better.

This is an appropriate point to identify a crucial issue in relation to social exclusion which is illustrated by a contradiction in the Liberal Democrat's examination of the general issue. They identify two very different minorities in their discussion. The first is a minority who have gained by social change, a minority located at the top of society and separated from the rest of us by increasing and heritable relative advantage. There is considerable evidence to support the existence of a separation of the ever more affluent few from the remaining static or actually becoming poorer many. However, social exclusion as generally discussed is not about the emmiseration of the many, of the majority. It is about a 'sloughed off' minority at the bottom of society separated by material poverty and increasingly distinguished by negative cultural characteristics. These people are not just poorer. They are different. There is much less evidence for a clear division downwards in terms of permanent condition. On the contrary, as we might expect if the poorest are a functional reserve army for post-industrial capitalism, there is considerable dynamism with people moving into and out of material destitution and in and out of the segregated socio-spatial zones of exclusion, although much of the dynamism of the system occurs with relatively limited income movements by people who remain fixed in space.

If we consider exclusion to be about material circumstances, then the degree of dynamic change in those circumstances over time makes the notion of a permanently segregated underclass absurd. The spatial evidence seems to tell a somewhat different story. We shall find evidence of the polarization of urban space in post-industrial capitalism, but of a polarization in which the very poor and the not quite so poor live in the same areas with considerable mobility within those areas between those statuses in contrast with the 'respectable' spaces which continue to display the social relations and forms of the Fordist era. There is some mobility between those two sorts of areas over time for individuals and households. Material exclusion is very real, but for most of the excluded it is a status which can be escaped from, just as for most of the non-excluded it is a status which always threatens by its presence.

Exclusion from power is a very different matter. Power is the most nebulous and most important of all social concepts. Measuring it is almost impossible. We tend to use proxies in terms of the consequences of the possession of power, measured usually by measures of material circumstances. In post-industrial capitalism the actual ability of the mass to influence political process is much less than it was under industrial capitalism. We really can talk about the exclusion of the many to the advantage of the few. The politics of urban development and urban policy provide a very clear illustration of this process. More directly the constraints imposed on the capacity of unions to act at the point of production by the legislative underpinnings of flexible capitalism, are crucial to the disempowering of ordinary people.

Let me make absolutely explicit something which is inherent in the account of the development of post-industrial capitalism presented thus far. My argument is that advanced industrial societies are converging on a norm of social politics organized around a flexible labour market and structural social exclusion. One interpretation of the general post-Fordist account, which can be mechanistic, is that such a convergence is an inevitable consequence of the logic of contemporary capitalist accumulation, that base is determining superstructure. I actually think that kind of mechanistic Marxism for capitalism's interests, what Cleaver (1979) calls 'mere political economy', is wrong and that the convergence is very much driven by the ideology of liberal capitalism, by the manipulation of political processes, and by the subordination of policies to business interests. None the less convergence is happening. Gorzelak (1996) puts this well for the Polish case:

> It has been generally assumed that the changes occurring in the post-socialist countries result almost entirely from a shift from the centrally planned economic system supported by a mono-party regime to a market economy introduced in a democratic political system. This approach stresses the 'ideological' or systemic factors in post-socialist transformation . . . If this approach is correct, the post-socialist transformation should be regarded as a unique phenomenon, specific only to the transformation from a communist (or so called 'real socialism') system to a market economy . . . However, even simple reflection reveals that these assumptions do not hold true. In fact, the restructuring processes that dominate in the post-socialist transformation very strongly resemble the phenomena which shaped economic life in more advanced Western countries since the 1960s and specially during the 1970s . . . With a great deal of simplification one may say that the post-socialist transformation is a shift from Fordist to post-Fordist type of organisation of economic, social and political life. This shift was not possible in a closed system, separated by economic and political barriers from global markets and therefore not exposed to economic and political international competition. Once these barriers were removed, the old patterns of economic production could no longer be maintained and 'imported' patterns of new ways of socio-economic and political organisation begun [sic] to shape the new reality.
>
> (Gorzelak 1996: 32–3)

It is true of course that we can easily identify the agencies which are forcing this sort of transition in Poland. They are the employers of what Poles call the Marriotski, since these people jet into Warsaw, stay at the Marriot Hotel, and instruct the Poles as to how to reconstruct their economy and their society. However, we have to accept that this process is having an impact everywhere. There has been a massive industry of examination of different welfare regimes which has developed following Esping-Andersen's (1990) interesting book on that topic. It is ironic that this interest has become an academic growth industry at just the time when global pressures, which are primarily ideological although they are represented as inevitable tendencies in the only possible reality, are leading to a massive reordering of all welfare regimes which do not prioritize labour flexibility. As we shall see, a consideration of complex social dynamics shows us that another social order is possible, but the flexible and excluding version is the one which is being made for all of us if things go on as they are

The one thing which all commentators agree on, whatever their views on the desirability and/or inevitability of the kind of new social order which has come into being, is that there has been a qualitative change. Things are not the same as before – in the language of complexity/chaos we have experienced a phase shift at the level of social order. Let us now turn to a research programme which is exploring the implications of that shift for individual lives.

The complex dynamics of social exclusion

> Past theories, essentially static in form, are challenged by new ways of thinking.
>
> (Leisering and Walker 1998a: xiv)

Leisering and Walker's important collection *The Dynamics of Modern Society* (1998a) is representative of a very rapidly developing programme of dynamic analysis which derives from the availability of longitudinally ordered data sets in which the trajectories of individuals and households can be followed through time by repeated remeasurement of the character of those individuals and households at regular intervals. This is not a new programme. The oldest still continuing UK longitudinal study is that initiated by J.W.B. Douglas in 1946 which is still pursuing the life trajectories of those born in one week of March of that year. However, the more recent studies, typified by the British Household Panel Survey, return to remeasure at much more regular intervals and tend to be household focused rather than dealing with individuals (see Leisering and Walker 1998a).

The difference between the earlier cohort studies and the new longitudinal studies is not the product of arbitrary whim. Although Douglas's study was originally concerned with paediatric health, it rapidly became focused on educational attainment and social mobility. The study was embedded within a conception of life courses which reflected the social realities of the Fordist era, in which people were not absolutely fixed or ascribed by their circumstances of birth, despite the continuing significance of those circumstances. Instead there was a considerable degree of upwards social mobility, often but not invariably mediated through educational attainment, which reflected the changing occupational structure of developing Fordism with its growth in more desirable white collar employment locales. The tradition of mobility studies, typified in the UK by the Nuffield programme (see Erikson and Goldthorpe 1992), was one which looked at change but conceptualized such changes as essentially single. People started off in one position and either stayed there or moved, but there was really only one key transition.

Although this conceptualization did fit the general reality of the Fordist era, it was a simplification even then. Now it is wholly inappropriate. Although many people do have relatively stable life trajectories, the proportion of those who do not, whose lives involve repeated personal phase shifts to radically different circumstances, is very much greater. The great value of the dynamic approach to longitudinal studies is that it enables us to chart the character of such shifts for very large ensembles of individual trajectories.

Leisering and Walker (1998b) locate this new tradition precisely in relation to the phase shift in the whole social order described in the previous section of this chapter. They present an essentially Schumpeterian view of the inherent character of modernity:

> the dynamism of modern society resides in novel institutions that display an intrinsic propensity to continued and unlimited change. It is this propensity, and not change as such, that we refer to as dynamism.
>
> (Leisering and Walker 1998b: 4)

It is important to make absolutely explicit something which these authors do note in later discussion. One reading of their account of dynamism would present us with an understanding of change as a continuing and on-going process, a process which could be described by ratio scale measurement of conditions. This is essentially the approach of time ordered studies in economics. Leisering and Walker do recognize that social dynamism does not take this form, but that it instead involves abrupt qualitative changes. Their important discussion of changes of regimes of inequality (Leisering and Walker 1998b: 6) is exactly an account of qualitative change, of phase shift. This point is crucially important.

The weakness of the dynamic tradition as it has so far developed derives from the micro character of the data sets on which it is founded. This is well illustrated by the empirical part of the Leisering and Walker (1998a) collection. The three substantive empirical sections contain a series of interesting and important chapters which are about the dynamics of people within societies, not about the dynamics of society understood as an emergent reality – for a realist there certainly is 'such a thing as society'. The development of dynamic perspectives, using the enormous macroscopic range provided by longitudinal data sets,[2] enables us to chart life courses, but we have to set those life courses within the complex and non-linear dynamics of changes in the whole social order and changes in socio-spatial systems which are contained within that social order.

These accounts are crucial to any understanding of the character of social exclusion in post-industrial society, precisely because such exclusion must have a time component. At its simplest this time component is duration. Short spells of poor condition can be handled quite well if these are set within a life trajectory which includes spells of better conditions. Indeed if we look at income alone we might find some people who measured at a point in time had no income at all at that point, had quite high incomes and good standards of living if we used a different accounting period. This could be true of, for example, very highly paid freelance media personnel, who might have a flow of income very different from that of a salaried person.

More seriously we need to establish if there are types of trajectory which might describe categorized sets of experience. Within the set of such sets, we might find one which describes the dynamic experience of social exclusion.[3] The obvious one is long term unemployment with dependency on low level benefits. However, we might well find, and indeed will find, that a set of individual/household trajectories which involve low paid work as the normal experience with considerable experience of unemployment punctuating such low paid work, is much more significant and represents the most significant kind of excluded life in our sort of society.

Is there a way to integrate the micro level accounts of individual life trajectories with the macro level of categorical or phase shift transformations? I shall argue that there is and that it is provided by the perspectives of complexity/chaos theory to which we shall now turn.

Understanding the complexity of dynamics

The best way to present a short account of the chaos/complexity perspective (see Byrne 1998 for a fully developed account) is by picking up the implications of the idea of multidimensionality and considering what happens when one of the multiplicity of dimensions is time. Poverty is a unidimensional concept. It is measured traditionally by comparing material resources possessed by a household, that is the unit of ultimate consumption which may contain only one individual,[4] with some standard which is either absolute and biologically determined or which reflects the prevailing social norms of the (usually national) society within which the household exists. The measurement takes the form of a financial summary, usually expressed in terms of income over a specific time period. Much of the evidence about poverty comes from snapshots, from studies conducted at one point in time. Even at the beginning of poverty studies there was an alternative understanding of dynamism. Rowntree identified his cycle of poverty in the early 1900s (see Townsend 1979) by looking at how a working class family's ratio of resources to needs was likely to move them below and above a poverty line at different demographic stages during the family's life. We can think of the time line of individuals and households as being the life course. In a multidimensional treatment we do not consider and measure just one attribute over time as poverty studies measure income. We measure whatever we think is significant. These measurements are the coordinates on a set of dimensions which constitute a multidimensional state space. If we measure a household's income, size, housing tenure, employment relation (say through an operationalization of Pahl's (1984) conception of work rich – work poor: see Byrne 1995), educational connection, cultural level and health state, then we have seven dimensions on which we have scores. We can use numerical taxonomy procedures to generate a typology based on these measures and we can allocate cases to the categories which constitute this typology. If we measure the variables at different points in time then we can plot the path, the trajectory, of the household as it changes over time. We can see both if there are changes in the nature of the social typologies and explore the movements of individual cases among the types in the typologies. The state space is the space through which we plot these changes over time, not just for one case but for a multiplicity of cases, for what in chaos/complexity theory is usually called an ensemble.

In most real systems, and in this example each individual household constitutes a system, some changes are not gradual and incremental. Rather they are sudden and discontinuous. They are not linear but non-linear. For example the loss of employment produces a non-linear change in economic circumstances whereas a wage rise produces only a linear change. It is the non-linear, qualitative, changes which matter to us. Most of the empirical chapters in Leisering and Walker (1998a) are about non-linear changes in the life courses of individuals and households. We must also accept the reality of changes in the actual social categories which constitute the social domain within which individual and household life courses are conducted.

The idea that duration of condition is crucial to understanding the social implications of any set of circumstances is plainly sensible. The idea has been implicit in benefit systems for many years and was taken up as an explicit theme in the USA by David Ellwood (see Leisering and Walker 1998). The theme is developed in many of the pieces in Room's (1995) edited collection dealing with 'the measurement and analysis of social exclusion'. However, this dynamic literature had tended to see discontinuous changes, the phase shifts, as nothing more than the boundaries of duration. The full implication of such non-linear boundaries has not been appreciated.

To understand why that should be so we need to examine not individual cases but many cases, to look at the ensemble of trajectories. If we do we find that as we map trajectories through time we do not find either an even or a random patterning of trajectories throughout the condition space. Instead we shall find certain areas of the condition space being occupied with sets of trajectories which, while they are not the same cycle on cycle, none the less stay within particular boundaries. The term used for such bounded domains is 'attractor'. For a single trajectory the attractor is the limited part of the phase space within which it is contained. It is useful to think about the situation for ensembles of trajectories which have similar attractor paths. In other words if we map all the trajectories in the condition space we find subsets of the whole ensemble in particular and different parts of the condition space. The use of numerical taxonomy procedures is a convenient way of identifying exactly these ensembles of attractors.

We are also likely to find instances where a case moves from one bounded set in the condition space to another, with that movement being determined by a change in one or more key control parameters which set its location in the condition space. For example a benefit dependent female single parent establishes a new cohabiting relationship with an employed man with reasonable earnings, finds it worthwhile to take a part-time job herself, on the basis of the new combined household income moves from a poorly regarded social housing area to medium priced owner-occupied housing and experiences all the consequences – including perhaps more successful schools for her children – which are associated with that spatial change. This is a discontinuous change of kind.

If we look at the set of trajectories which move over time within a bounded part of the condition space, we can (I think) realize that the set is more than the simple aggregation of its individual components. Morris and Scott (1996) are among the most recent of the many critics who have noted that a crucial failing of much quantitative sociology is the nominalist fallacy. In particular, social class is understood in much sociological work as simply a property which is possessed by individual cases. On the contrary, class is an emergent phenomenon which is the product of the interactions of its component parts. It has a reality over and beyond any individual component and has causal powers which do not derive from the properties of those components taken separately. The whole debate about spatial concentration and possible consequent deviant cultures (see Byrne 1995 for a summary) is about such emergence.

However, people and households do not have life courses which are somehow separable from the society of which they are a part. Let us think of the social order of industrial capitalism as taking the form of bounded trajectory, a torus, which has undergone a non-linear change and which now has a new and different bounded trajectory. I have previously described this as taking the form of a butterfly attractor (Byrne 1997a) in which there are two domains rather than the single domain of the torus.[5] People lead their own lives, but not in circumstances over which they have complete control. The kinds of changes which are summarily described in this book as constituting the phase shift from industrial to post-industrial capitalism mean that the sorts of lives available to be led have changed. Of crucial significance here is the elimination of a middle income lifestyle based on relatively well paid male manual work supplemented by not badly paid female industrial or other work. There is a dynamic and non-linear trajectory for the social order as a whole. The system of society which has undergone non-linear change surrounds and contains the systems of individual life courses.

There are other levels of dynamic change. Spaces have dynamic trajectories. The globalization thesis is an account of the dynamic trajectory of the whole social world in space. There is an extensive spatial literature about the dynamic changes for regions and localities within that global space. Here the spatial level which will be considered most carefully is that of neighbourhoods within city regions considered as containing systems. In other words we have a multiple set of nested systems. This idea is due to Harvey and Reed (1994). They conceptualize a series of systems in which, to use our example, the global social order contains regions which in turn contain localities which in turn contain neighbourhoods which in turn contain households which in turn contain individuals. It is very important to note that in this approach there is no hierarchy of influence. Causal processes can run in both directions. None the less, it seems obvious that grand global changes and changes in the socio-spatial organization of the regions and cities and neighbourhoods within which people live, have enormous influence on the possibilities available to them for developing a life course.

The idea of chaotic/complex change, as opposed to the idea of catastrophic non-linear change in which there is a qualitative transformation but only one new sort of trajectory is possible, contains within it the idea of not one sort of possible future but of different sorts of possible futures – the plural is crucial. This is the idea of bifurcation. In science chaos is not a synonym for randomness. Chaotic processes are wholly deterministic. The problem is that small differences in initial condition produce very different outcomes as the system moves through time. In their seminal book on these topics Prigogine and Stengers (1985) noted that in social systems where there was the possibility of reflexive social agency, that agency might be what makes the difference. At the level of the individual/household, action can change life course. At the level of the whole social order, collective intervention can change the social system. In other words the kind of miserable, divided, excluding post-industrial system, which seems to be becoming generalized on a world scale, is not the only form of social order available to us. Different actions might produce different outcomes. At last we have a glimpse of hope!

The concept of 'control parameters' is very important here. We have already employed this idea in relation to the causes of changes in the character of the trajectories of individuals or households. In essence the term describes the way in which non-linear qualitative changes in the character of systems which are described in a multivariate way are often not the product of changes in the values of all the parameters describing that system. System transformation may result from changes in a very limited number of those parameters, often only one of them. We shall see that for single parents the establishment of a two parent household can be such a crucial change. This applies equally to whole social systems. Of particular significance for us will be the idea that the degree of inequality in a social system is a control parameter for its form. Highly unequal social orders generate the attractor state of social exclusion. More equal social orders do not have this attractor state.

There are three key points which emerge from the preceding discussion. The first is that 'social exclusion' is an emergent phenomenon which is constituted by the interaction among the life courses of the ensemble of individuals and households who for varying periods of time occupy a separated part of the condition space describing possible life courses, which part is defined by categorically worse conditions as measured on a multidimensional basis. In other words 'social exclusion' is not a label to be applied to particular 'socially excluded' individuals and/or households. We must get beyond nominalism.

The second is that the existence of this separate domain is a product of changes in the character of the social order as a whole. Contemporary social exclusion is a product of the phase shift in the character of contemporary capitalism. It is an inherent property of polarized post-industial capitalism. In this context the significance of age cohort is of particular importance. Those who established much of the basis of their life courses under a previous and more equal social order will be much less affected than those whose life courses are established under the new and less equal social order. The young cannot carry forward the advantages of Fordism, other than what they may inherit as assets from their parents. Finally, to express in a very preliminary way something that will be crucial for the conclusion to this book, we must carefully distinguish between actions which change the trajectories of individuals and/or households in terms of shifting them across attractors within a given condition space, and actions which change the character of the condition space and the attractor sets available within it. We shall find policies which move people from excluded to non-excluded, while leaving exclusion as a domain. The real issue is how to get rid of the domain, how to create a social order which excludes exclusion.

Chapters 5 and 6 examine the dynamics of social change at the macro level and consequent micro trajectories, as these are expressed in two ways which are crucial for any understanding of social exclusion. Chapter 5 deals with changes in income. Here the macro level is changes in the form of the income distribution of whole societies and the micro level is the actual trajectories of households around the income distributions of those societies. Chapter 6 examines changes in the socio-spatial systems which constitute urban spaces. Here we shall examine again the macro level of the global reconstitution of space, the meso level changes in the socio-spatial systems of particular urban spaces, and, to the extent that we can, the actual trajectories of households around these socio-spatial systems.

The chapters are not merely descriptive. They seek to establish the complex causal processes, including the very significant proactive effects of fiscal and benefit systems on income distributions and trajectories and of urban planning and development on socio-spatial systems and spatial trajectories. Moreover they are not simply retrospective; they do not say just what has happened and why, but begin to explore what might happen in the future if things go on as they are. In the Conclusion we consider how things might be done differently and the potential for a different social order which might be created by such different social action.

The dynamics of income inequality

Income inequality matters in any consideration of social exclusion because income is both the basis of social participation through consumption and a reflection of the power of people in their economic roles. The general tendency in advanced capitalism during the Keynesian era was for income inequalities to get smaller (Goodman *et al.* 1997). The people and households who were poorest became better off relative to the rest of us. That has changed and it is important to understand just how it has changed and to see how both economic restructuring and changes in policy have interacted to produce more unequal and excluding societies.

In Chapter 4 we identified two aspects of the dynamics of income inequality. The first is at the macro level of the whole distribution of income within societies. We shall examine macro changes in the UK and USA since the 1970s for which we have rather good data, say something about Poland for which there are some data, and make some remarks on France for which there are fewer data available, at least in English. The second is the micro level of the trajectories of individual (and/or household) incomes over time. Again we have good data for the UK and USA because there are established longitudinal studies in those countries but we do not have equivalent dynamic studies for Poland and France. This chapter deals with each of these levels in turn. Having examined both the macro and the micro, the last part of the chapter reviews the way in which fiscal, benefit and industrial relations policies have played a proactive role in creating both interlinked domains of contemporary social life.

From relative equality to inequality: the phase shift in income distributions

There are three points to make before we begin the examination of changes in the character of income distributions. The first is about the nature of any changes we might identify. Studies of income distribution have generally been conducted within a frame of reference derived from the discipline of economics. Economics almost always works with continuous data supposedly measured at a level which corresponds to the full properties of general arithmetic. In other words changes are seen as incremental and smooth. The chaos/complexity approach suggests that what we really should be interested in when we examine any change over time is not incremental change but rather sudden and abrupt discontinuities, non-linearities, qualitative changes. Marx put this rather well when he suggested that such changes involved a transformation of quantity into quality. The question is whether or not income distributions have changed in such a way as to produce a qualitatively different kind of social order?[1]

The second thing we must consider is the relationship between the forms of income distribution in societies and the class structures of those societies. Income is never irrelevant to any theoretical scheme of class within sociology, but it is really central only to Weberian approaches in which differentiated income is the basis of differentiated consumption.[2] This book is informed by a generally Marxist perspective but I agree absolutely with Westergaard when, having defined class very broadly as 'a set of social divisions that arise from a society's economic organisation' (1995: 1) he remarks:

> it is my aim precisely to clear away any assumption that close attention to distributive benefit and disadvantage is inherently out of tune with Marxism; and to uphold instead the contention . . . that the consequences of unequal economic distribution by way of unequal personal experiences and prospects in life must be central to class analysis of whatever theoretical persuasion.
>
> (Westergaard 1995: 4)

As Westergaard notes, actual empirical studies of inequality pay so much attention to income because it is easily operationalized and there are many income distribution data available. In contrast power is extraordinarily difficult to operationalize and there are no data available. Perhaps this is one of the reasons why contemporary discussions of social inequality place so much emphasis on consumption, again a measurable thing both in quantitative and qualitative terms. Hence the emphasis on consumption as the domain of agency in contrast to the processes by which social orders are created which are much more difficult to access.

There is a deal more to class than just income, but it will do as a dimension around which to explore inequalities. Interestingly it is rather easier to explore income inequalities by other crucial dimensions of inequality; race/ethnicity, gender and age, than it is by class, precisely because they are operationalized independently of income. Here changes in income inequalities by race/ethnicity, gender and age will be examined, again with the focus on the UK and USA where there are relatively good data, although there are suggestive signs for Poland and France. It is worth noting that race/ethnicity and gender are principles around which legislative programmes, derived from the liberal conception of possessive individualism, have operated since the mid-1970s in both the USA and the UK. These programmes have reduced income inequalities by the categories of gender and race/ethnicity while income inequalities within the categories have substantially increased.[3]

Age is very interesting as a collective descriptor. Here attention will be paid, not to elderly people, who are so often poor, but whose low incomes are not part of the process of social exclusion *per se*, as to young people. If we have had a qualitative shift in the form of the social order, then we would expect its effects to be particularly apparent among the young who are entering the new social world, and in particular its employment system, *ab initio*.

When we examine distributions of cash as resource we need to consider both income and expenditure precisely because of the dynamic instability of income in societies with relative insecurity of condition. If we examine the data which come originally from the UK's *Family Expenditure Survey* and which cover income and expenditure in a given week, we find a dissonance between location in the distribution of expenditure and income.[4] The households in the lowest decile by income are not necessarily located in the lowest two deciles by expenditure. What this indicates is precisely the effect of the instability of incomes. People can smooth expenditure over periods longer than a week when they have irregular incomes to contend with (see Goodman *et al.* 1997: 6).

If we examine the pattern of changes in income inequality in the two societies in which public policy has actively promoted a flexible labour market, the UK and the USA, we find that since the late 1970s there has been a considerable increase in inequality. In the UK the real incomes of the lowest decile after housing costs were taken into account are now substantially below their real value of 1979,[5] having declined by some 25 per cent (see Goodman *et al.* 1997: 112). Whereas 'average' real incomes increased by 30 per cent between 1979 and 1990/91 in the UK, for households in the bottom half of the income distribution, real incomes increased by only about 10 per cent. The top decile of incomes in contrast saw an increase of more than 60 per cent (see Westergaard 1995: 132–3). Westergaard sums up the position thus:

> Even people up to mid-point incomes, and a number some way above that level, have gained quite little either by comparison with the rich or by past standards of rising prosperity. The poor are much less a minority by virtue of exclusion from benefit of radical-right market boom than are the wealthy by virtue of high-boosted privilege from it.
>
> (Westergaard 1995: 133)

Hills (1995: 40) has examined the changing shape of income distribution in the UK between 1979 and 1990/91. There are two interesting aspects to this. One is the separation between households with no full-time earners and those with full-time earners. Over the period the modal income of the former set has become much less than that of the latter set, having previously been rather close to it. The second is the shift in the distribution for those households which do have full-time workers. This has become much more spread out with large disparities and an emerging bimodal form. This inequality of earned income matters a great deal because it is the simplest direct indicator of an overall change in the level of inequality in the social order. That level is a key control parameter determining the form of actual social order, from a range of possible social orders, which will exist.

The origins of this increased inequality, and of the changing characteristics of the poor, are unequivocally identified by Goodman *et al.*:

> The emergence of mass unemployment has had a major effect on the income distribution. Families with children now make up more than half of the poorest decile group compared with only around a third three decades ago, with the main reason for this change being the increase in unemployment between the early 1960s and the mid 1980s.
>
> (Goodman *et al.* 1997: 112)

However, in the United States unemployment in the mid-1990s is actually less than it was in the 1960s. What has happened to income distribution in that society?

Developments in the USA have been comprehensively reviewed by Braun in a book with the interesting title of *The Rich Get Richer* (1997). The crucial factor is the decline in real wages for most people in the bottom two-thirds of the income distribution. Braun, drawing on US Bureau of Labor Statistics, puts it like this:

> since reaching its peak in 1972–1973 real average weekly earnings have fallen by nearly 19 percent through December of 1994 . . . The average American worker is worse off today than at any time in the past third of a century. In terms of real earnings, today's typical worker actually earns less pay than workers did in 1960.
>
> (Braun 1997: 222)

In contrast to these declining real wages, profits have never been higher in US business running in 1994 at more than twice the average rate for 1952–79 (Braun 1997: 188). In 1992 almost one-sixth of US workers fell into the US Census Bureau definition of working poor and earned less than $13,091 in that year (Braun 1997: 238). The size of this group had increased by a third since 1979. In the USA the poorest fifth of households saw a 13 per cent drop in real income over the period 1973 to 1992. Over the same period the top fifth of the income distribution saw an increase of 11 per cent (Braun 1997: 257). Braun quotes figures from the Congressional Budget Office which demonstrate that the wealthiest 1 per cent of the US population has nearly as much after-tax income as the bottom 40 per cent and that the top fifth in the US income distribution receives as much income as the bottom four-fifths (Braun 1997: 263). It is extremely important to note that these inequalities have developed across the whole gender/ethnicity structure of the USA, although the relative position of ethnic minorities as compared with non-hispanic whites has worsened. At the same time gender inequalities have diminished.

Braun accounts for these developments in terms of the impact of global competition on the US economy but that argument seems poorly focused in important respects. The new international division of labour has led to a massive deindustrialization, particularly in the mid-West, which as Braun (1997: 367) notes has had particularly dire consequences for white working class males. However, he implicitly assumes a kind of common national interest which links working-class interests to higher service class interests and the interests of the owners of capital, when he writes of a US interest as such. In reality US capital has done very well and has been able to do so because insecurity, global restructuring and the disempowering of organized labour have enabled it to increase domestic rates of exploitation while maintaining effective nearly full employment.[6] Nelson's (1995) discussion of 'post-industrial capitalism' (see Chapter 3) explains very precisely how this has been done through both economic and political intervention by large corporations. The ideological hegemony of classic free market liberalism in US politics provides a covering gloss on extreme intervention and manipulation. In the UK New Labour is peddling the same sort of line, while acting as the rather open creature of global corporate interests. Crucial to the politics of post-industrial flexibility is the use of legislation to destroy the organizational capacities of workers at the point of production.

The effect on the 'class' structure of US society has been marked. In an article with the title 'The incredible shrinking middle class' Duncan *et al.* (1992) have reviewed income panel data since the mid-1970s. They define the middle class as households the incomes of which (adjusted for size) lie between two times and six times the US government's defined poverty line. Over the period from the 1970s until the late 1980s the proportion of US households in this range declined from 75 per cent to 68 per cent with a more marked decline for households containing children. This change reflected the complex and combined effects of significant movement from the upper middle to upper class, an even larger downward movement from the skilled working class component of this 'middle group' into the poor, and the effects of the recomposition of family structure. Duncan *et al.* (1992) conclude their review thus:

> The good news is that late twentieth century America has offered abundant opportunity for the upper-middle class. The bad news is that at the same time, it has reduced upward mobility among the working class and produced persistently high poverty rates for families

with children. These two opposing forces are draining America's middle class.

(Duncan *et al.* 1992: 38)

What is happening in Poland and France? When considering the Polish situation it is important to bear in mind Gorzelak's (1996) argument, quoted in Chapter 4, to the effect that what is happening in Poland is not different from the transitions experienced in the west. It is simply the same thing speeded up. What have been the effects on income distribution in Poland?

Weclawowicz (1996: 95) quotes from Domanskia (1994: 55) and shows that a substantial gap has opened up in the pattern of incomes in Poland. In 1978 the average monthly income per person in households headed by 'managers and higher state administration officials' was 145 to a national average of 100. In 1993 it was 317 to a national average of 100. In other words the relative incomes of the top group had gone from 1.5 times the norm to more than 3 times the norm. The non-technical intelligentsia have not done badly either with their relative incomes rising from 1.5 times the norm to 2.3 times the norm over the same period. All manual worker groups in industry and agriculture and peasants as a category saw a fall in relative incomes. Skilled workers who had had per person household income of 0.95 'the national norm in 1978' saw this fall to 0.79 in 1993. The fall for all other manual categories was even greater.

Weclawowicz (1996) considers that:

> It seems that the formation of three large social groups is under way: the elite, the middle class and the poverty class. The elite group will be constructed from the former communist elite or nomenclatura members, part of the former anti-communist opposition, and the intelligentsia. In very rare cases members of the former working class or peasants will be recruited to this elite . . . The middle-class group will be formed from former communist upper- and lower-grade nomenklatura, part of the anti-communist opposition leaders, and from the intelligentsia. The upgrading of the majority of the working class will be strongly limited because of the delay in the Mass Privatisation Programme, and by their low skill levels, maintenance of passive attitudes and a sense of claim or dependence on the state . . . The poverty group is emerging from all social categories losing from the transformation. Above all, it concerns the unemployed, some of the unskilled workers, the majority of the rural population (particularly former peasant workers), and owners of small farms, and even part of the lower-level intelligentsia. A large segment of the unskilled working class will also be on the loser side. This also concerns the majority of elderly people.

(Weclawowicz 1996: 96–7)

He argues that 'The working class had been struggling with communism for what could be called "socialism with a human face" . . . Instead of re-structured socialism, liberal capitalism has now been imposed' (Weclawowicz

1996: 100). Gorzelak (1996) describes the consequences. In contrast with the period of 'real socialism' when unemployment did not officially exist, by 1994 there were very nearly 3 million unemployed in Poland, i.e. 16 per cent of the civilian economically active population. It is important to note that only 550,000 of these were unemployed as a consequence of redundancy (Gorzelak 1996: 28). Many of the unemployed were young people coming from secondary technical schools and failing to get jobs in the contracting industries for which they had trained. Non-recruitment of the young coupled with job defence by those in work is of enormous significance in Poland.

There is a important, if implicit, difference of emphasis between the accounts advanced by Gorzelak and Weclawowicz. The former gives a structuralist account. It is restructuring which has caused the problems in Poland and this has to be understood in terms of the imposition of the post-Fordist logic of capitalist accumulation facilitated by the re-creation of a reserve army. In contrast, although appreciating perfectly the character of restructuring, Weclawowicz turns the focus onto the socio/political/cultural deficiencies of the Polish working class which, having brought down communism through collective action, remains remarkably reluctant to accept its new role as the flexible labour force of a post-Fordist liberal capitalism. This is rather well illustrated by the condition of the Polish coal industry centred on the Katowice industrial district in Upper Silesia. Here the miners, who were both the favoured aristocrats of 'real socialist' labour and a key part of the Solidarity opposition to 'real socialism', have often managed to retain their jobs thus far in the face of a threatened restructuring to the extent that coal output has fallen far more than employment. Contrast that with the 1960s restructuring of the UK coal industry in which employment fell by two-thirds and production fell by only about 20 per cent.

In terms of political views and objectives it is clear that the Manchester liberal programme of classical political economy which informs the ideas described in Chapter 1 has only a very limited constituency in Poland. What is popular is the social market model endorsed by conservative Christian Democracy as described in Chapter 2. The original ideology of Polish policy development as expressed in the Balcerowicz programme was explicitly neoliberal. However, there were some important contradictions in the actual process of implementation. This was indicated by the appointment of Jacek Kuron, a well regarded leftist opponent of the communist state, to the post of Minister of Labour and Social Policy, in the first, and several subsequent, post-communist governments. It is important to note that there has been a substantial development of Polish social insurance schemes and a massive increase in the proportion of gross domestic product (GDP) devoted to income maintenance programmes. In 1992 17.5 per cent of GDP was spent on such programmes, which was double the 1989 proportion (see Inglot 1995: 362).

The French situation is also complicated. Yérez del Castillo (1994) remarks that 'social exclusion' as a political issue is closely associated with strong feelings of social insecurity which are general in French society. For example 55 per cent of all French adults and 69 per cent of those in the age bracket 18–24 were afraid of losing their job at a time when French capital was increasing profits on the basis of employment reduction (1994: 619). Martin (1996) gives a similar account remarking that poverty is now

> a menace threatening all those working in the competitive sector, all those who cannot rely on long-term established posts, a kind of sword of Damocles hanging over wage-earners . . . the distinction between the excluded and the integrated person became somewhat blurred. Whereas formerly each individual had a specific profile, clearly identifiable characteristics, each one belonging to a different 'social world', henceforth the new feature was that one moved imperceptibly from one situation to another, rather like a sideways movement, a skid, a slippage, as a result of some event which disturbed the expected social trajectory.
>
> (Martin 1996: 384)

Atkinson *et al.* (1995) have examined income distribution in a range of OECD countries. For France they examined changes only between the years 1979 and 1984, which is not particularly useful for consideration of the contemporary situation. During this period while the incomes of the top decile in France rose relative to the median, the bottom decile's income remained relatively much more stable than was the case for the UK.

France has been marked by real popular and general social resistance to the tendencies of post-industrial capitalism. There have been occupations of benefit and employment offices, mass demonstrations, and a coherent social critique of the logic of flexibility. The Communist and Green elements in the ruling coalition have explicitly distanced themselves from any endorsement of 'Blairism' and are associated with radical Catholic elements, including a bishop suspended from office by the Pope, in a programme of active analysis of and resistance to globalization as a process. There are organizational examples here which we will consider again in the conclusion. Let us turn to a consideration of income distribution and its concomitants in relation to gender.

Gender and income inequality

Anybody's position in any social structure is complicated by the effects of collectivities to which they belong. We are used to thinking of this as an issue for women because we have a notion of women as 'dependent' members of households to which they are not the main economic contributors. The massive growth in female employment in post-industrial capitalism has changed all that. The resources in a household have implications for everybody in the household, whether male or female, adult or child. However, dependency does remain significant and gendered (for adults).

Dependency is a crucial issue. At one extreme it can be argued, from a possessive individualist position, that all adults must be treated as separate individuals. In the UK the introduction of separate assessment for income tax purposes works on this principle to the great advantages of affluent households. In contrast poor benefit dependent women are subject to a household test for incomes which actually predicates against them maintaining a legal relationship with their partners (see Parker 1989). If we do look at 'own right' incomes then only about one-third of adult women in the UK, almost all in full-time employment, have incomes higher than levels usually used to assess poverty.

There is considerable evidence of unequal resource distribution by gender within households, although it must be noted that much of this is somewhat dated and that the 'degendering' of social relations in general are likely to have had an impact on the pattern of intra-household resource distribution.[7] However, studies which ignore this intra-household distribution, itself the product of complex and differentiated patterns of resource acquisition and allocation, and simply regard households as undifferentiated social atoms, are not describing social reality as it is. Likewise, the treatment of individuals as social atoms, regardless of the resources of the household to which they belong, is an invalid approach to social reality as it is. The only possible approach which would adequately address this issue would be a study based on detailed contemporary patterns of internal resource allocation in all forms. This is necessary but it is not going to be done here. Instead I am going to focus on the group of women who are the least complex to assess and who are often unequivocally socially excluded – single mothers.

There are two reasons for doing this. One is that the single mother is the limiting case of female dependency. There is no 'dominant' permanently resident male and the single mother acquires with motherhood all the liabilities of care which cause difficulties for full-time economic engagement, plus the liability to maintain her own dependent child or children.[8] The other is that we need to address the new conservatism's obsession with the single mother as the generative mechanism of welfare dependency and underclass status. Overarching both these is the reality that many, if not all, single mothers and their children are plainly poor. I am going to use the position of single mothers as a basis for discussing arguments about the feminization of poverty in the societies being considered. Let me say straight away that here we shall find differentiation both among societies and within them. The evidence is that in the UK poverty is less female than it was under Fordism/industrial capitalism, although there are far more poor women. In Poland the proportion of the poor who are female has risen. This is also true of the USA, where 52 per cent of poor families were female headed in 1989 compared with 23 per cent in 1959 (Rodgers 1994: 31).[9] In the last case, we find, as we shall find again with ethnicity, a clear differentiation developing within the gender category. This is also a crucial phenomenon in the UK. Kodias and Jones (1991) put this well:

the slight improvements registered for women in general actually represent substantial gains made by a minority of women, primarily in the professions, and static or deteriorating circumstances for the majority of women who need to work.

(Kodias and Jones 1991: 161)

Let us first try to sort out causality. There are two causal accounts which argue that single parenthood is a generative mechanism for poverty. The first we might call 'weak and demographic'. This sort of account is not about the assignation of blame nor does it argue that children's experience of single parenting *per se* does them any damage. It is a demographic/epidemiological account rather than one of causation for individuals. Essentially it is based on the recognition that households headed by female single parents are likely to be poor. If there is a growth in the proportion of such households in a society, then there will be a growth in poverty/social exclusion which will take the form of a feminization of poverty because both the absolute numbers and proportion of the poor who are in female headed households will grow.

There is an immediate statistically reflexive problem. If we see a growth in the time series in both poverty/social exclusion and female headed single parent households we are observing merely correlation. Correlation is not cause. We can argue, and indeed should argue, that the causal chain may well be in the other direction: poverty/social exclusion, based on the reduction of the wage earning capacity of men, may well be causing households to be headed by female single parents. Given the existence of such reflexive relationships the use of linear modelling techniques is always problematic, but Kodias and Jones (1991) conclude on their examination of US evidence that

female-family formation explains only the pool, and not the poverty, of female families. Our analyses do show a strong relationship between family formation dynamics and female poverty growth. Beyond this, however, economic changes at the local level were found to be of significance. Growth in women's employment and the expanding female service sector were the most important correlates of female-family poverty growth in metropolitan areas. It is indeed ironic that the service sector, which provided the greatest increase in women's employment over the decade, is so strongly associated with female poverty. No support was found for the argument often advanced by conservatives, that welfare expansion is positively related to female poverty.

(Kodias and Jones 1991: 169)

This last point is of particular significance. The neo-conservatives, whose ideas were discussed in Chapter 1 and who are represented in the UK by Green (1998) drawing on the ideas of Mead (1997), argue that the availability of benefits promotes single parenthood. In the more extreme forms, as expressed by Murray (1990), and in the crude version of the 'culture of poverty' benefit dependent single parenthood is the generative mechanism for a lifetime trajectory of dependency and 'underclass' status, not only for the mothers but also for their children who lack the model of the male wage earner and perpetuate the poor female headed family in their own reproduction. This old and lousy tune is the strong programme. Rowlingson and McKay's (1998) study of the dynamics of lone parenthood in the UK offers some interesting qualitatively derived findings which are relevant here. These authors conclude that:

> the growth of lone parenthood has occurred partly because of two sets of circumstances. For single women from poor backgrounds who get pregnant, lone motherhood is a relatively attractive option beside the alternatives of living with a poor man or staying as a single woman with a poor job. For women in couples with children, a different situation applies. These women are no longer so constrained, by economic necessity and social norms, to remain 'for better or worse' in a traditional two parent family.
>
> (Rowlingson and McKay 1998: 206)

Some spatial data can cast some light on the actual causal mechanisms operating. In a study of Leicester as a divided city I found (Byrne 1997a) that there was a marked and emergent difference in the legitimacy status of children born to mothers with addresses in the affluent two-thirds and poor one-third of that historically prosperous locality. In the affluent areas 96 per cent of all children were born to parents who were married. In the poor areas less than 50 per cent of children were born to parents who were married, although the largest category of unmarried parents jointly registered their children from the same address. The emergence of the social divisions in Leicester were clearly established as originating in the deindustrialization of the locality. The growth in 'non-married' births, and the spatial pattern of such births, can be identified as a consequence of the same processes over the same period. This picture very much supports Rowlingson and McKay's (1998) general account given above.

The US experience is dispiriting. Kodias and Jones (1991) argue that the cause of poverty for female headed families in the USA is not welfare dependency but rather the labour market positions available to them and forced upon them in a context where, as Orloff (1996) puts it: 'the US is moving to require paid work as the only route for the support of households, whether headed by couples or single mothers' (Orloff 1996: 55). So is the UK. This fits exactly of course with the logic of post-industrial capitalism as described by Nelson (1995) (see Chapter 3).

The general character of evidence does not support a simple monocausal account of the feminization of social exclusion/poverty. Grolowska-Leder and Warzywoda-Kruszynska's (1997) conclusion based on their study of the Polish industrial cities of Lodz and Katowice is actually generally applicable:

> No matter if in Lodz or Katowice there are virtually the same types of households that are likely to be pushed into poverty. These families

can be described as families with dependent children, households with low economic resources, broken families, and families with insufficient welfare cover. Families at risk of poverty among female headed households seem to be gender specific modifications of types that are found in the whole sample . . . The only exceptions that could be held to be a gender specific pattern are households with divorced women. It is rather unlikely for men to be placed in financial underprivileged situation after divorce . . . Though underlying factors that make females unable to support their families are the same as in other segments of the large industrial urban community, women tend to be more vulnerable to be slipped into poverty.

(Grolowska-Leder and Warzywoda-Kruszynska 1997: 11)

Race/ethnicity and exclusion

When we turn to considerations of exclusion by ethnicity the limiting case is provided by the historical experience of black US citizens.

Until the 1960s, black Americans were virtually excluded from full and equal civil, social, and political citizenship rights accorded to the white native-born population and to naturalized immigrants. Thus, the boundaries excluding them were foremost racial, reinforced by social, economic, and political segregation. In the 1980s, blacks have gained formal citizenship equality. Yet, only middle class, and to a lesser extent working-class blacks have been able to benefit from the new legal equality. The economically weakest members of the black population remain excluded. The boundaries that exclude them are primarily socio-economic and secondarily racial. The socio-economic dimension reflects the limited nature and institutionalization of social citizenship in the United States.

(Heisler 1991: 468)

Ethnicity is intimately linked with citizenship but different from it. The formal citizenship of black Americans was established with the emancipation of the slaves, but it took the Civil Rights movement of the 1950s and 1960s to turn it into anything approximating a reality. Catholics were nominal citizens in Northern Ireland but a series of explicit mechanisms excluded them from the rights of citizens in a 'Protestant state for a Protestant people' at the provincial level, while, and ironically, the 'imperial' rights of citizenship of the colonizing power were fully available to them, and the imperial mechanisms were not discriminatory in employment and service provision.

In industrial and post-industrial capitalism there is an additional confounding factor. Ethnicity is often associated with immigrant status. The two things are not the same. Neither Northern Ireland Catholics nor US blacks are immigrants in any meaningful sense. However, many (in the UK most) ethnically differentiated people are immigrants or the descendants of recent immigrants. In the UK almost all immigrants were effective citizens on arrival, but in the USA this is not the case for Latinos who form the significant part of recent immigration in relation to any discussion of social exclusion.

What position do people occupy in the system of stratification in the social order, if we look at their position by ethnicity? Note that there are two fixes on this. One, which underpins UK and US anti-discriminatory legislation, is individualistic and reflects the dominant motif of possessive individualism. We might see it as having achieved its objectives when ethnicity is essentially irrelevant to social position. This is becoming the case for example for people who self-classify as 'Indian' in the UK (Peach 1997). The other is collectivist and considers overall position of the those who self-identify with the group as a whole.[10] Essentially the second position is founded on group solidarity.

There are marked differences among the societies which are the basis of illustration in this book. Both the UK and the USA are multi-ethnic societies on a somewhat different scale, although the UK is much more multi-ethnic if the Irish descended are considered as an ethnic minority. In Poland, which before the Second World War was a complex and multi-ethnic society, the tides of world history and the criminal lunacies of the Nazi era, finished off by residual Polish anti-Semitism, have produced an effectively homogeneous population, although observation suggests that the Rom (gypsies) remain as a disadvantaged and significant group. France is a multi-ethnic society with a history of ex-colonial immigration similar to that of the UK but with a more restrictive approach to the allocation of citizenship rights. Despite France, UK and USA's common status as multi-ethnic, the implications of ethnic minority status are very different in the three societies as a whole, and within them are very different for different groups.

In the USA the key, continuing aspect of ethnic exclusion is represented by the position of black Americans, and this exclusion is generated by the continuing significance of the central residual element of the racism founded on the forms of chattel slavery, the continuing reality of ethnic segregation to a unique and intense degree of black from white Americans. This is a matter of racism rather than simple ethnic differentiation. The 'one drop of blood' basis for the identification of black Americans as not white – one drop of 'black blood' made someone black under the race codes which existed in many US states until the 1950s – was racially excluding rather than involving any of the cultural dimensions which are so significant for ethnic differentiation.

The situation in the UK is rather different from that in the USA. First, there is no specifically disadvantaged 'other than White' group.[11] Rather there are series of ethnicities with very different social relations surrounding them. Indeed those who identify as black are the least separated from the UK white population. Peach (1996) notes that:

> The Black Caribbean population's position in Britain stands out in strong contrast to that of African Americans in the USA. Its structure

is more working class than the population as a whole, but it does not differ dramatically in terms of housing tenure, jobs or residential segregation from the white population. It has an exceptionally high proportion of mixed Black and White households and in this way appears as the most integrated group.

(Peach 1996: 23)

Peach's remark forms part of the introduction to a four-volume series describing *Ethnicity in the 1991 Census* (1996, 1997) which provide the most complete and up to date review of the situation of the UK's ethnic minorities. The experiences are very different. In the fourth volume Karn (1997) summarizes the overall position thus:

A particularly important point emerged in relation to occupations and lifestyles. *Within* each ethnic group there was a strong relationship between occupational level and lifestyle. However, *across* the ethnic groups, occupational level had far less influence on the quality of lifestyle. Other factors were contributing to the differentiation of the groups and giving advantage to the Whites. The same factors appear to have influenced the incidence of unemployment.

(Karn 1997: 281, original emphases)

In other words, at all occupational levels there is a real disadvantage for 'other than White' ethnic minorities as compared with 'Whites' in their own occupational category.[12] However, there are very different locations in relation to the overall social structure. People who self-classify as 'Indian' are on the whole somewhat better located in the social order than 'Whites' as a whole. All other large ethnic minorities are not, with Pakistanis and Bangladeshis being particularly disadvantaged.

The exclusion of the young in post-industrial capitalism

What can we say about the general position of young people in these post-industrial capitalisms? Let us remember the point made at the beginning of this chapter that if the social order changes, then the people who begin key phases in their lives subsequent to those changes will find that their lives are very different from those whose lives were set on track in an earlier era.

Hills (1995) summarizes the findings of the Rowntree Foundation's investigation of these issues, noting that: 'the stakes are higher for younger cohorts: as they enter the labour market, the difference between those who do well (linked to high qualifications) and those who do not is much greater than it was for those entering the labour market twenty – or even ten – years earlier' (Hills 1995: 48). Green, A. (1997) shows that 39 per cent of workers aged between 25 and 34 have experienced at least one episode of unemployment in their working lives. This is by far the highest rate for any age group. People with between 9 and 18 years in the labour market are

25 per cent more likely to have experienced unemployment than those with 30–50 years' exposure to the risk. There is very clearly an age related effect here which shows the considerable significance of cohort experience. Those who entered the labour market as it has become post-Fordist experience the disadvantages of that directly. Those with a history of work under Fordism retain some of the advantages of that system.

Changes in the UK have been particular dramatic. MacDonald (1997) notes that:

> In 1974 when Paul Willis's lads . . . were stepping from school into manual, working-class jobs, their counterparts in Teesside were doing the same; finding apprenticeships and jobs at British Steel, ICI or the docks. Then, 55 per cent of Teesside's 16 year olds left school for employment. Within twenty years, the movement of the area's school leavers into work has virtually ceased. In 1994, 4 per cent got jobs; the lowest figure ever recorded. Youth Training now soaks up about a quarter of the age cohort (with only around one-third of these finding employment afterwards). Further education has become the dominant structure through which post-16 transitions are made: in 1994, 57 per cent 'stayed on' compared with 28 per cent in 1974. In 1994, 16 per cent of the cohort were 'unemployed'.
>
> (MacDonald 1997: 21)

Teesside, one of the most 'deindustrialized' locales in the UK (see Byrne 1995), is a limiting case, but the trends are general. If we look at the composition of the 1994 cohort of school leavers we see that about one-third of the cohort (those 'unemployed' and the two-thirds of Youth Training Scheme (YTS) trainees who do not find employment) are plainly starting on a trajectory which is going to be relatively worse throughout their working lives. The proportion in this category will undoubtedly be larger since some of the entrants to employment and to further education will also join this category. We can see the signs of a bifurcation.

The Polish situation is also dramatic. In urban industrial centres union pressure has often been effective in sustaining the jobs of those who already had them, but the mechanisms of transmission into work have broken down. There was in Poland a system of technical schools associated with particular industries and often with particular enterprises which channelled young adults directly into work. The collapse of recruitment meant that in 1993, 31 per cent of all Poland's unemployed persons were in the age group 18–24 (Weclawowicz 1996: 145). The problems that this poses are likely to be exacerbated by demographic factors which will inject even more young adults into the labour market. Educational differentiation is now emerging as a crucial factor in Poland. This is associated with both an expansion of state higher education and the development of a private (and semi-private) system of, in particular, business schools. Actually the educational developments in Poland seem singularly suited to the provision of the divided labour force required for many post-industrial enterprises.

The US experience indicates that long term developments are not to be understood in terms simply of a poorly educated helotry and an educated class with good and increasing levels of resource control. On the contrary, although there is a clear 'education premium' in lifetime earnings, Braun (1997: 230) shows that real wages for college graduates have declined since 1987, albeit at a lesser rate than for non-graduates.

An important question which emerges from the development of qualification founded social division, a social division exactly commensurate with the employment structure of post-industrial capitalism, is whether or not this is generating a cultural divide? Mead's (1997) insistence on the need to orientate welfare programmes towards workfare, to make welfare receipt conditional not on confinement in the panopticon of the workhouse, but on labour in a workhouse generalized to the society as a whole, is of course predicated not just on Benthamite utilitarianism, but also on a belief that a culture of anti-work exists among the citizen poor. Bluntly put, they want too much and will not put up with very little. The actual ethnographic evidence from the UK does not support this view. Indeed security seems to be more important than wage levels. If anything I think MacDonald (1997) is overestimating the aspirations of the dispossessed young when he summarizes the implications of the range of studies included in his edited collection:

> There was one, inescapable conclusion which cut across all these studies. Both young people and adults wanted work. They would fail with flying colours the test Murray sets to prove the underclass's existence: 'offer them jobs at a generous wage for unskilled labour and see what happens' . . . They were extraordinarily dogged and enterprising in their search for work amidst the economic wreckage of their local labour market. They remained attached to remarkably durable, mainstream attitudes which valued work as a key source of self-respect, as the principal definer of personal identity, as a social (and in many cases moral) duty, as the foundation upon which to build sustainable family lives and respectable futures.
>
> (MacDonald 1997: 195)

The only thing wrong with that is that, in my experience, young people do not need generous wages to induce them to work. They will work for any gain above benefit level. As someone who entered the labour market in the 1960s and remembers the contempt for exploitation which people could express under conditions of full employment, it seems plain to me that my older child's generation have lost something very real indeed.

However, MacDonald's (1997) own study, while a convincing account of the situation of marginalized young people on Teesside, is not a complete account of young people's work experiences in even that limiting case of the social consequences of deindustrialization. There is another sort of work experience for the young which is predicated upon high level qualifications and entry into another kind of labour market. However, this is not a work experience of historical advantage. The young adults with good formal qualifications who enter this labour market are relatively advantaged compared with the dispossessed working class. They are disadvantaged compared with their own parents.

This situation is well illustrated by the North East of England's fastest growing new industry – call centres. This is the top end of the labour market of post-industrial capitalism. Although there is a gender bias in the tele-sales and customer-services complexes in that the staff of call centres are predominantly female, there is an element of degendering and young men also work in these occupations. The gender issue will be who proceeds to managerial positions. These jobs are clean, secure, require a good general education (many entrants are graduates) and are in contemporary terms relatively well paid, although they certainly do not offer a 'family wage'. They are remarkably supervised and managed, a superb illustration of the reality, contra Bauman's (1998: 25) assertion, of the continued significance of the 'panoptical drill' in modern society. There is a distinction between employment in this field and employment in the field of dispossession, but it is not a distinction of exemption from gross exploitation and powerlessness at the point of production. The main distinction is stability, although call centres may actually be rendered obsolete very quickly by the development of Internet based information and purchase systems.

The implications of social bifurcation for young people need spelling out carefully. The evidence is not for a situation in which some young people are much worse of than their parental generation of the Fordist era, and some are better off, with the divide being something on the lines of half and half. Rather it is for a threefold division. There is a large dispossessed and casualized poor. There is a large better qualified and better remunerated in contemporary terms, but historically downwardly mobile educated proletariat. Finally, there is a category, most of whom are inheriting privilege but some of whom are entrants from below, who get into the higher reaches of the service class as managers and private sector professionals. It is this elite whose situation is better. We seem to be developing a something less than 10 per cent, 50 per cent, 40 per cent society under post-industrial conditions.

Dynamics: the significance of life courses

Let us turn to what the longitudinal studies show us about the actual experience of life courses in the closing years of the twentieth century. The development of dynamic studies has provided ammunition for the right. Pryke (1995) (who is 'right' perhaps only in the sense that his unpolemical and data driven pamphlet is published by the right wing think-tank, the IEA) notes that if we examine the conclusions of the most important recent UK study of income distribution, that conducted by Hills (1995) for Rowntree, we find that Hills's

own estimates indeed suggest that when money income is measured
on an annual basis, the top ten per cent are six time richer than the
bottom twenty per cent but that when income is measured over a
lifetime, the top decile has only two and a half times as much income
as the bottom quintile.

(Pryke 1995: 22)

Pryke is perfectly correct in his interpretation of the Rowntree study. However, it is very important to remember that any lifetime data available in
the 1990s describe the lifetime experience of those whose life course trajectories have been for most of their adult lives under the conditions of Fordism.
The whole point about the discussion of the phase shift from Fordism to
post-Fordism is that future trajectories are likely to be very different.

There are two sets of studies which utilize data dealing with experiences
under post-Fordist conditions. The first is one using data derived from the
US Panel Study of Income Dynamics (PSID). Here Ashworth *et al.* (1994)
examined the life courses with regard to childhood experience of poverty
(defined in terms about 25 per cent more generous than the official US
poverty line), of all children in the panel born between 1968 and 1972. The
period examined was the first 15 years of life. Although the authors do not
use the language of complex dynamics, what they describe is a set of seven
sets of trajectories. One group, comprising 62 per cent of the sample, never
experienced poverty. Of those who did more than half had a childhood of
spells of poverty, punctuated by periods of moving out of poverty, although
given the linear and single dimensional definition of poverty we do not
know by how much. Just over a quarter experienced only one spell of poverty
of less than one year's duration. The rest experienced long spells of poverty
or were always poor. The findings of this study certainly support the
notion that the important group are those whose lives are characterized by
movement to and from poverty, although we do not know the extent of
the movement.

Hill *et al.* (1998) have examined poverty processes in young adulthood
using a sample derived from the PSID study who were aged between 8 and
13 in 1968. They use a linear model approach for analysis, with all the
disadvantages of such techniques. The predictors of poverty transitions in
young adulthood are personal behaviour, especially in relation to educational
success and marriage/childbearing patterns and parental background. Hill
et al. (1998) note that: 'the evidence of background being mediated by
behaviours is weak, except . . . when the behaviours are taken to extremes'
(1998: 99). This is distinctly pessimistic and supports an account of closure
of mobility opportunities.

The second set of longitudinal studies are those based on the British
Household Panel Survey (BHPS), which was first undertaken in 1991.
Goodman *et al.* (1997) examined household income movements for those
who were in the bottom quintile of income distribution during the first three
passes of this study in 1991, 1992 and 1993. Again the measure employed is

the single dimensional one of income, with quintile being necessarily an arbitrary cut-off point on a continuous measure. Nearly half of those who were in the bottom quintile in wave one were there in both waves two and three. Of those who escaped between wave one and wave two, more than half made it only into the second quintile, so changes in income may have been marginal (see Goodman *et al.* 1997: 257–64). The categories of household most likely to escape the bottom quintile at some point comprised couples with no children and single people with no children (some of whom may well have been students who moved into work). The category least likely to escape was single parents with children.

Gosling *et al.* (1997) have used BHPS data to examine the relationship between low pay and unemployment, a crucial issue for the general description of post-industrial capitalism which is endorsed in this book. They have used data from the first four passes and note that while two-thirds of all men aged between 18 and 60 and economically active in the sample were in full-time work continuously between 1991 and 1994, just 9 per cent were permanently unemployed during this period. In other words nearly a quarter of men experienced episodic unemployment. So far as the relationship between wages and unemployment goes, their conclusions are unequivocal, if, as they remark, hardly surprising:

> lower relative wages of individuals are associated with a higher probability that they will move out of work in the future. Among men over thirty per cent of those starting in the bottom quarter of the wage distribution spent some time out of work in the next two and a half years. This was true of just twelve per cent of those starting in the top quarter of the distribution. Similarly, looking at transitions into work 56 per cent of the men moving out of unemployment moved into a job with wages in the bottom quartile of the distribution . . . movements into and out of work are overwhelmingly experienced by those who can obtain only rather low wages.
>
> (Goodman *et al.* 1997: 1–2)

Rowlingson and McKay (1998) and McKay (1998) have used BHPS data to examine the dynamics of lone parenthood. Here the crucial shifts are the entering of the condition by childbearing or break-up of partnership and leaving it by establishing a new partnership. McKay's conclusion that

> Early lone parenthood appears not to be the result of rising labour market participation, but of growing inequality of opportunity among young women. Key factors are a disadvantaged background and low participation in education.
>
> (McKay 1998: 122)

supports the account of polarization of experience among the young argued for here.

The BHPS data are available for only a few years, although as the results of successive passes become available we shall be able to engaged in proper explorations, ideally employing multidimensional categorical techniques at successive time periods (see Byrne 1998), in order to see what exactly are sets of trajectories of individual life courses, under the conditions of post-industrial capitalism. The findings which are currently available, as with their US equivalents, support absolutely the general account of active under-development advanced in Chapter 3. Let us turn to the role of policy in this process.

Making it unequal: the role of post-industrial policy

Social policy as a field of academic study has traditionally been concerned with the way that welfare systems distribute resources around the social structure. Sociology, and more recently geography, have had a disciplinary focus on the way in which the basal character of the social structure, by which is almost invariably meant the mode of production, however complex and qualified the description of that mode, 'determines' the character of welfare systems. Certainly there is scope for agency and contingency, hence the general interest across the social sciences in the idea of typologies of welfare regimes as originally developed by Esping-Andersen (1990). However, base is seen as determinant, even if the use of the word 'determine' is the sophisticated version suggested by Williams (1980), that is to say the setting of limits. Westergaard (1978, 1995) has written about this in a most pertinent way. If the logic of welfare reform transcends the basis rules of capital accumulation, and in particular if it seeks to create equality on the one hand and challenges the notion that ownership represents a valid claim on social product on the other, then boundaries are being tested indeed.

All the above is true, but it is very far from being the whole truth. Welfare systems are not merely determined products of basal social order. There is an absolute and interactive reflexivity between the social arrangements of welfare, understood both as institutional forms and systems of distribution, and the social order. If the form of the mode of production (always capitalism of course, but available in variants and marked by categorical transformations – changes of form which represent a difference of kind) limits and causes welfare, then welfare systems limit and cause the forms of production. Systems of welfare, understood in the broadest terms, are constitutive of the social order just as much as the arrangements of production.

With a vocabulary from chaos/complexity theory available to us, we can conceptualize the whole thing in a most useful way. We have to see mode of production as not simply the organization of the process of production. It must include all aspects of social reproduction. In chaos/complexity terms we have a far from equilibric system defined by boundaries and constituted not by simple unidirectional causal processes, but by complex, reflexive and interactive causal processes.

The implications of this are enormous. Most accounts begin with a description of processes of production. Regulation theory is absolutely characteristic here. Fordism is first a system of production. The mode of regulation is seen as a product of that system of production. There is no sense of necessary interaction. There are of course exceptions to this. Radical history of the early phase of industrial capitalism in the UK, in particular the work of E.P. Thompson (1963), always recognized that the Poor Law was not simply a product of the generalization of wage labour relations under a factory system, but an absolutely necessary precondition for their generalization. This was true enough for England but it was absolutely fundamental for the mobilization of the Irish as the flexible element in nineteenth-century English and Scottish capitalism. The contemporary significance of the argument that social policies are constitutive lies in the ways in which a range of social policies make flexible post-industrial capitalism possible. Without them it could not be. They are fundamental to it. The development of Welfare to Work as an alternative to insurance based wage substitution rights is simply the most recent, if also perhaps most important, development in a programme across the range of social policy which can best be understood as facilitating flexible post-industrialism. The implications of this new scheme will be elaborated in a moment, but a brief preliminary consideration here will illustrate the general argument.

Under principles of solidarism, as influenced by Keynesian specifications of the effective range of macro-economic policies, citizenship rights included the right to work. Note the difference between a right to work and an obligation to work. The right to work was a right to work of a kind which could be interpreted as acceptable in terms of a solidaristic definition of 'good work'. If such work was not available, and the offer of such work was the test of entitlement for those not working but fit to do so, then there was a right to wage substitution benefits paid at a solidaristic level. This remains the social/Christian democratic norm. The obligation was on those with the power to manage the system. They had the task of making work available to the potential workers. Solutions had to be demand led. Welfare to Work is supply side. The interpretation is that workers do not have work because they are defective, not morally or even rationally as was the understanding in the early nineteenth-century heyday of tutoring utilitarianism, but in terms of personal deficits. The obligation is imposed on them to redress these deficits, as a condition of benefit, in order to make themselves fit for labour. There is no specification of the conditions of that labour as having to represent 'good work'. The logic of the employment form of much of post-industrial capitalism is that the work will not be good work. However, people have to be made to do it, and in the personal services sector which is not exportable, domestic labour (or immigrants without rights) have to be made ready to take on these tasks. Welfare to Work is a constitutive process for this.

The constitutive effects of welfare do not merely relate to the conditions and circumstances of the dispossessed. The allocation of large personal resources to the affluent through the reduction of their taxation levels is an essential precondition for the growth of the privatized consumption which is so central to post-industrial capitalism. Likewise the recasting in the UK of the form of state education away from egalitarianism, and towards family mediated individual achievement, is constitutive for the differentiating processes shaping personal trajectory towards adult life. On the consumption side, the role of post-industrial planning in the shaping of differentiated urban space, is another key constitutive element. In the rest of this chapter we shall look at UK and US fiscal and benefit policies as constitutive processes for post-industrial capitalism.

Speenhamland and the new enclosure: taxation, benefits and Welfare to Work

In 1795 the magistrates of the English county of Berkshire concluded at a Newbury quarter sessions that wages were no longer sufficient 'to support an industrious man and his family'. A meeting was called at the Pelican Inn in the parish of Speenhamland and there a policy was worked out which resulted in the subsidizing of labourers' wages from the poor rates on a sliding scale depending on family size and the price of bread (see Inglis 1972: 81). The resultant 'Speenhamland' system was simply the best known of a range of similar locally developed schemes devised around this time, but became the generic term for all of them.

The background to these developments was complex. In part it was a function of enclosure. The elimination of common rights turned the cottager into a pure wage labourer. In part it was a function of rising prices in consequence of the French wars. In part it was a function of economic competition by factories against domestic labour. The development of factory spinning eliminated a significant source of income generated by the labourer's wife and children. The family was being transformed from an economic resource into an economic burden.

The magistracy was drawn from the English gentry, a class composed of as hard-faced a bunch of rural capitalist exploiters as has ever been assembled anywhere at any time. They were influenced to some degree by moral motives, but their prime concern was the collective as opposed to individual interests of capitalists as a class. At the local level they were, as Marx put it, acting as the executive committee of the whole bourgeoisie. Every individual capitalist farmer wanted to pay as low wages as possible. If such low wages were paid there was no guarantee of the long term reproduction of labour, since labourers would avoid marriage and the production of children. In the short term there would be a seasonal problem of labour required at harvests, since additional labour was always drawn from families at these times. The magistrates devised a workable scheme for handling these problems, which scheme persisted until the introduction of machine threshing reduced the long term demand for agricultural labour in general, and resulted in the New Poor Law. It should be noted that this later transition was also dependent on the extraordinarily severe suppression of workers' resistance and efforts at union organization (see Hudson 1981 [1910]).

There is a very important parallel to be drawn between this period of transformation and the present. Enclosure represented a massive transfer of common resources to the rich. It was legal robbery sustained by the law which 'hangs the man and flogs the woman that steals the goose from off the common, but leaves the greater villain loose that steals the common from the goose' (Anon.). The poor were emmiserated thereby: 'The affluence of the rich supposes the indigence of the many'. As Heilbroner (1993: 27) reminds us: 'It is Adam Smith speaking, not Karl Marx'. The parallel with today is enormous. In 'flexible capitalism' we can see massive resource transfers to the most affluent, the capitalists and the comprador new superclass, including many and possibly most politicians. This transfer is mediated not only by changes in employment and remuneration, but also by taxation and benefit policies which in combination represent a transfer of public resources on a major scale. This transfer, I am going to argue, represents a new enclosure, an appropriation of the commons for the benefit of the few at the expense of the many.

The political theory of possessive individualism was developed by Locke as a way of establishing a defined set of personal freedoms against domination by feudal and post-feudal elites. It was a revolutionary doctrine and underpinned two real revolutions which matter a great deal in the trajectory to modernity, the American and the French. It was not a doctrine founded to separate the interests of the individual from that of the community of the individual's peers. It was intended to define the freedom of the individual against the superior lord. Of course in the Anglo-American world it became the justification precisely for elite appropriation of the commons. In Britain the elite was, ironically, drawn in large part from the old nobility and from Celtic chieftains transformed into nobles.

I am all for the reappropriation of the commons, but more immediately want to consider the revenues of tax as 'common' by an, undeniably radical, extension of Titmuss's idea of the fiscal component of the tripartite division of welfare. Titmuss (1958) argued that a tax exemption granted to support a specific social purpose must be regarded as exactly equivalent to a direct public expenditure for any specific purpose. Forgone taxation was just as much a cost to the public revenue as any monetary expenditure funded from those revenues. Titmuss, however, confined fiscal expenditure to tax allowances which always were hypothecated, i.e. had a specific and identifiable purpose. My proposal is that we should regard any cuts in taxation which apply not generally, but rather to the benefit of a particular social group, as a fiscal grant, even when these are not tied to any hypothecation. The basic understanding is that in welfare capitalism the public revenues represent the commons which are the birthright of all, and that giving up large chunks of them to the most affluent can be understood as exactly equivalent to enclosure.

This account equates a tax cut with a benefit increase so we have to examine carefully the way in which taxes and benefit interact. This examination is made rather difficult by the shift, in the UK in particular, from taxation of incomes and wealth to taxation of consumption. Indirect taxes are generally considered to bear harder on the poor, unless they are targeted specifically on luxury goods. There are no comprehensive studies I can locate of the impact of the shift to consumption, but Kempson (1996) provides a reasonable impressionistic summary:

> Since many poor people pay little or no direct taxes, it might be thought that fiscal changes would affect their lives very little. But the shift from direct to indirect taxation has meant that people living on low incomes now carry a higher tax burden than they did ten or fifteen years ago. And the reforms of local taxation have, in many cases, added to that burden. Both these changes have had a disproportionate effect on people whose incomes have risen least over that period, – people on fixed, low incomes and those dependent on social security for their income.
>
> (Kempson 1996: 129)

The discussion that follows is based on shifts in direct taxation and benefit levels. However, in considering the pattern of those we must never forget that the shift to taxation of consumption has meant that the real level of resources available to poor people, the post-indirect tax consumption, is actually worse than the pattern revealed by those shifts.

In the UK the pattern of taxation has been quite radically revised by massive reductions in the higher rates:

> Income tax rates have been reduced markedly since 1977–78, particularly for those on higher incomes. The basic rate fell progressively from 33 per cent in April 1978 to 25 per cent in April 1988, and in 1992–93 a new lower rate of 20 per cent was introduced. The higher tax rates, which rose to a maximum of 83 per cent on earned income, have been replaced by one 40 per cent rate.
>
> (*Social Trends* 1995: 89)

UK direct taxation does remain progressive, even though most taxpayers pay tax only at the standard rate. This is because of the existence of a system of allowances which means that the average rate of tax is not the same as the marginal rate across the wide range of incomes on which standard rate only is payable. However, the progressive element is much less than it used to be, particularly when income tax and national insurance are taken together.

Treatments of the effect of taxation on the distribution of income can take two forms, that based on 'actual payments' and that based on the 'what if' approach. Goodman *et al.* (1997) explain the nature of these approaches and summarize their implications:

The Jenkins study (based on the 'actual payments' approach) answers the question 'how much redistribution is the tax system doing now compared with a decade ago?' The answer to this is that it is doing about as much in the late 1980s as in the late 1970s. This is because the pre-tax distribution has become much more unequal, and so even with lower tax rates, the tax system is still doing plenty of redistribution. The Johnson and Webb study based on 'what if' approach is answering the question 'what would the post-tax distribution look like if the tax system had not been changed?', and the answer is 'much less unequal'.

(Goodman *et al.* 1997: 206)

It is very important to note that this kind of account considers only the implication of the tax take, not of the consequences for tax funded public expenditure. In other words the account of the distribution of income is based only on the higher incomes having less with no consideration of the consequences of spending the tax take on those with lower incomes, either as direct transfer payments or in kind.

Hills (1995) makes the point somewhat more strongly:

Without discretionary change, the direct tax system would have 'worked harder' and slowed the growth of inequality after 1978. In fact, substantial discretionary changes in direct tax structure have almost precisely offset the automatic effects, so that growth in inequality of post-tax incomes has matched that in gross incomes.

(Hills 1995: 61)

In the United States the situation is even worse. Hills's comparative examination of income distribution led him to conclude that: 'In the USA taxes and transfers accelerated the effect of a widening distribution of market incomes: discretionary policy changes more that offset the automatic reaction to rising market inequalities' (Hills 1995: 72). This kind of development was not inevitable. In France and Canada over the same period discretionary changes in tax and transfers operated as negative feedback and effectively cancelled out a rise in original market income inequality (Hills 1995: 72). Duncan *et al.* (1993) in a review of the causes of the 'shrinking middle class' in the USA conclude that:

we consider it vital to continue to re-examine the Federal income tax and to reconsider wealth taxation – in particular capital gains taxation at time of death or transfer – as a source of meeting America's human resource needs. Because the fruits of American economic growth are increasingly being concentrated among the privileged 10–15 per cent of the population at the top of the middle-age income and wealth distribution, serious consideration should be given to a modest sharing of this wealth.

(Duncan *et al.* 1993: 264)

Duncan *et al.*'s proposals are indeed modest. They argue for a raising of the top rate of US federal taxation from 35 to 37 per cent and for a refundable child tax credit, of much more value to earners who pay low or no tax than an allowance. They also argue for targeted labour market policies intended to raise the qualification level of the low skilled. Their reference to wealth is of considerable importance. Reduction in wealth taxes in both the UK and the USA have made the inheritance of position and privilege even more important as a determinant of life trajectory at the upper end of the income scale.

If we turn to the level of transfer payments in the UK we find that the shift to uprating these only in line with retail price inflation and not in line with wages has contributed to the development of income inequalities. The increase in child benefit in the 'Welfare to Work' budget of 1998 was an equalizing measure, but it was the only direct income transfer of significance for almost twenty years.

The reduction in the taxation of the affluent is a key factor in the reduction of the level of services in kind across the board. There are arguments that the absolute level of such services has been maintained, at least as measured by real expenditure upon them, but this is not the general public perception. That perception is of a decline in relation both to overall national income and in relation to need. Certainly this is the general experience in relation to services provided in the UK by local government. This matters for two reasons. First, the provision of public services in kind is an important universalizing measure. The other side of public services is that they represent an alternative form of job creation to the traditional Keynesian macro focus of industrial production, which is now far less effective because of the combined effect of productivity gains and internationalization of production, and meso focus of infrastructure public works, again now far less job rich because of productivity gains. Social value derives from workers in health, social care, education and a range of other public services. Cuts in higher tax rates reduce or eliminate the prospect for the employment in the public service, where there remains a trade union based capacity for defence to some degree of the conditions, if not remuneration of work. The affluent are left free to spend on themselves alone and do so in the growing sector of post-industrial services, many of which are the products of privatization of the public sphere. The situation of workers in that sector is much worse than that of public employees.

In Poland it is clear that large-scale tax evasion in the informal sector is a major element in the development of income inequalities but there is a special problem which is typical of the experiences of post-communist societies. In Poland in general and in Upper Silesia in particular, many public services were provided in whole or in part by enterprises. This was not uniquely communist. It was in fact quite characteristic of carboniferous capitalism in general in western Europe as well. Even if the enterprises have not closed, as many have, they no longer are necessarily either directly providing or paying for public services of all kinds, including health clinics, social welfare services, subsidies to technical education and recreational facilities.

However, Poland has not seen a fall in overall social spending. On the contrary (although cuts in enterprise provision are not factored into this account) Inglot (1995: 362) notes that: 'we witnessed an unprecedented expansion of social expenditure in proportion to the Gross Domestic Product'. Between 1989 and 1992 social expenditure doubled as a proportion of GDP. In particular expenditure on pensions was increased in response to political pressure with pensions being used as a way of easing the pain of industrial contraction. In general the post-communist history of transfer payments in Poland shows the significance of real political pressures from below, which in any event accord with the actual, if somewhat undeveloped theoretically, solidaristic ideologies of the main political forces in the country.

Let us turn to 'Welfare to Work', the new policy programme of liberalizing US and UK governments committed to the development and sustaining of flexible labour markets. In the UK Gordon Brown's budget of 1998 was specifically identified as concerned with exactly the promotion of welfare to work. Critics, not least the former Tory Chancellor of the Exchequer Kenneth Clarke, noted that Brown had presented a budget with no macroeconomic content whatsoever. On the contrary the only remaining macroeconomic tool, the setting of interest rates, the 'one club' in the golfer's bag, had been handed over to a committee of the Bank of England drawn largely from the financial sector and including a US citizen who is a former CIA employee![13] There was no sense that part of the purpose of government financial policy was to stimulate demand in order to create employment.

All the innovations were institutional rather than systemic. They were intended to increase the return to employed work for people who had access only to low wages and to provide a set of incentives and supports for those for whom the alternatives were low wages or benefits. There was a radical reform of employers' national insurance contributions to encourage the hiring of more low-paid workers, a tax credit for the child care costs of parents with lower incomes, a US style working family tax credit which replaced and extended existing family credits, and a subsidy paid to employers who take on long term unemployed people. In addition there was a massive extension of counselling and training provision for all the non-employed poor. Credit packages also applied to disabled dependent people on benefit.

The thinking behind this approach was rather well explained in the first 'forecast for the UK economy' issued by the Treasury in 1997. This document was entitled *The Modernisation of Britain's Tax and Benefit System: Employment Opportunity in a Changing Labour Market* (HM Treasury 1997). The account given of the source of the problem here is accurate and exactly reproduces the account given at Speenhamland two hundred years ago:

Evidence on the dynamics of the labour market shows a clear link between unemployment and low pay. This low pay–no pay cycle means that, for many groups, income mobility is low. Relative poverty, defined as the proportion of the population living below half average income, is increasingly a problem for people below pension age, mainly through lack of work, but also through low pay. Many of those who suffer most are families with children.

(HM Treasury 1997: 2)

For the Treasury pundits, 'the focus of reform must be microeconomic' (1997: 17). It is true that they do recognize the significance of the macro-economic background but the key processes must be supply side and directed at the quality of labour. In the language of complex dynamics they are intended to move people between attractors, not to transform the phase state as a whole.

The effects of the 1998 Budget, coupled with the introduction of a minimum wage, will be very similar to those of the package introduced by President Clinton in the USA in 1996. The UK measures are not so coercive, yet, but in the USA the Welfare Act shifted long term responsibility for mothers with dependent children, the USA's only 'funded dependent group' of working age, to the states from the federal level, and imposed a time limit of two years on benefit receipt. This was sweetened by a rise in the minimum wage and a guarantee of protection of health benefits for workers who change or lose jobs.[14] The other main foundation of the Clinton welfare programme is the Earned Income Tax rebate, which exempts the working poor from income tax until their incomes are well above the poverty level. Martin Walker commented: 'the gap is clear in the Clinton ideology, between those in work, who receive the state's help, and the undeserving' (*Observer* 25 August 1996: 17).

What these schemes guarantee is subsistence wages, in relative terms of course, but not more than that. They are effectively Speenhamland come again. This programme has two beneficial effects for globalizing flexible capitalism. First, it subsidizes the wage costs of the apparently necessarily low wage service sectors of post-industrial capitalism. Note that these costs are borne by the rest of us, the middle income earners who have not had major tax breaks. The low paid do have higher net incomes, but this costs those employing them nothing. The costs are borne by the generality of middle income tax-payers, not the rich who have had big tax breaks. This is subsidized employment with the subsidies being horizontal transfers within the working class. Second, the programme maintains both the work ethic and the general social order. Work remunerated below the level of social reproduction, and at a level no better than state benefits, is corrosive of the work ethic. Rationally, people are 'stupid' to work for wages at such levels. Of course they do work for such wages because there are many trans-economic reasons for working, not least self-respect (although working while greatly exploited is of course not a source of self-respect). None the less, the actual logic of possessive individualism as expressed in economic rationality tells them they are daft for doing so. The restoration of the economic rationality of low paid work is important.

And work is a great source of social order. Wages provide an income without resource to crime. People who go to work rarely have the time, or energy, to be disorderly and criminal. The threat of job loss is an enormously important order-maintaining sanction. Note that these factors do not apply to work in the irregular economy. On the contrary the expansion of the irregular and marginal economy is a challenge to formal order. It is extremely interesting that the US experience has been one of job creation within the formal and order generating economy, rather than marginalization and the expansion of the irregular economy on the Latin American model. The UK is seeking to go the same way.

There remains the problem of jobs being available. The UK is uniquely disadvantaged here. The centrality of internationally traded financial services situated in a specific geographical location, the City of London, to the economy, coupled with the control of macro-economic policy given to the representatives of that sector, means that exchange rates are being maintained at a level which is very damaging for the industrial sector in general. Exporting is harder and there is a considerable inflow of competing imports. The result is that this sector does not have jobs on offer, a marked contrast with the USA where manufacturing has maintained its employment volume. As the last of the Keynesians, if a fairly right wing variant of the breed, the former Tory Chancellor Kenneth Clarke remarked, while verbally knocking Brown all over the House of Commons, that Welfare to Work is pretty pointless in those large parts of the UK where deindustrialization means that locally no jobs were available. Welfare to Work, Clarke noted, was meaningless when there was no work. He might have gone on to add that the constraints placed on public service employment by his government and his public expenditure targets, being maintained religiously by Labour in office, were one of the main reasons why work could not be created.

However, it seems entirely likely that Welfare to Work will have considerable success on the US model, although it will not work as well as in that rather more employment centred system where the Federal Reserve does pay attention to employment levels as well as interest rates. That it works will not be a good thing. The UK Low Pay Unit praised the measures, saying Brown that 'By allowing them to keep what they earn and support their families through their own pay packets he has given them back their dignity and self-respect' (*Guardian* 18 March 1998: 15). There is an element of truth in this, but the long term effect of these fiscal measures is that low pay will be even more institutionalized as an aspect of post-industrial capitalism, while the affluent who benefit as managers, service class workers, and owners of capital, will continue to enjoy the fruits of exploitation without paying much tax on them. Well, New Labour is definitely post-socialist.

Tax and benefit systems typically operate at the level of the nation state and affect life chances through their effect on income. We can explore their impact because we can measure their distributional effects, albeit with some difficulty! We have already noted Westergaard's (1995) reminder that we tend to study income streams and their distribution because they are more accessible than 'power', a nebulous thing which appears only in its use. I now want to turn to a domain of policy in which power is exercised, and in which the tendency especially in the UK but also in the USA has been to disempower citizens in general and poor citizens in particular, the processes for the management of the reconstitution of urban space – planning and urban development.

Divided spaces: social division in the post-industrial city

> today's 'underclass' . . . inhabit a space characterized by a
> deficit of economic, social and cultural regulation. In such
> spaces older organized capitalist social structures – industrial
> labour market, church and family networks, social welfare
> institutions, trade unions – have dissolved or at least moved
> out . . . unlike the spaces of the city centres and the suburbs
> they have not been replaced by the information and
> communicative structure.
>
> (Lash and Urry 1994: 8)

That urban society has become much more spatially polarized in consequence of the transition to a post-Fordist/post-industrial social order is a relatively conventional position. Marcuse (1989) has challenged the notion that there is a simple bipolar space with two separate kinds of social order within cities, but there is actually rather good empirical evidence to suggest that Lash and Urry (1994) are quite right in their general description of the emergent character of socio-spatial systems in post-industrial cities (see Byrne 1995, 1997a, 1998). Note that their account is one which fits very well with the idea of a bifurcation; the torus style space of the Fordist city (see Esser and Hirsch 1994) has become something qualitatively different with two very different types of social experiences predicated on distinctive areas of residence.

There is of course nothing new about the notion that cities are divided. Let alone the general account of the Chicago school (See Massey and Denton 1993), Engels (1968) recognized the extraordinary separateness of spatial life between the middle classes and the industrial proletariat in the Manchester of the mid-nineteenth century. However, the general tendency of the working-class project of respectability was towards the achievement of a social and spatial system in which, while inequality continued, its absolute range was much reduced and there were no dramatic and discontinuous breaks in the socio-spatial structure. The ideal-type of the urban for this project was represented by the British New Towns of the 1950s, but in general in metropolitan capitalism, with the single but enormously important exception of the black American ghetto, socio-spatial systems under Fordism were much less polarized than ever before.

That is not the case now. We can see this using multivariate measurements of the character of social space. We can appreciate it from qualitative interpretative research. Callaghan (1998) has shown how detailed knowledge of the socio-spatial divisions of an industrial city forms a crucial part of the repertoire of everyday knowledge of those who live in that city. We utilize it in the practices of our everyday life.

There are two very interesting aspects of socio-spatial division. The first is that, in contrast to division as expressed through household income, there is a rather sharp break located in the bottom half of the social order. With income the rich are separate from the rest of us. With space it is the poor who are separated off. Indeed spatial exclusion is the most visible and evident form of exclusion. We know the 'ghetto' estates of the cities in which we live. The second is that there is a double dynamic of space. The first dynamic, scarcely researched at all in the new project of dynamic empiricism, is the actual movement of households around social space, and in particular from the spaces of dispossession to those which are 'normal' and from the 'normal' to the spaces of dispossession. Indeed the actual expression of social mobility in terms of consumption is most marked precisely by change in area of residence. Callaghan's (1998) respondents actually envisaged their life courses as trajectories over time through the different residential spaces of the city in which they lived.

This is important because spatial location determines access to crucial social goods, and in particular to different kinds of state education, which have enormous significance for future life trajectory. In other words housing is not merely the largest element of privatized consumption and a crucial demarcator of lifestyle; for many people where they live determines what sort of schooling their children get and that determines much of their future life course. It is also extremely important for health, especially paediatric health.

The other dynamic trajectory is that of the character of social spaces themselves. The transition from an industrial to a post-industrial social order has been associated both with considerable gentrification of inner city working-class neighbourhoods, which gentrification is often the product of public policy, and in the UK and France with a transformation of social housing from being the zone of residence of the organized working class to its being, for younger households, the zone of residence of the poor and poorly employed.

Space is not merely a demarcator with regard to social exclusion. A very considerable part of public policy in Europe has been directed through space by being targeted on spatially defined 'communities' and particular blocks of land with a view to the regeneration of land and the reintegration (and sometimes, in rhetoric at least, the empowerment) of the people resident on that land. The trajectories of spaces are in large part the product exactly of urban policies in interaction with the effects of other social policies. The evidence is that urban regeneration, far from reintegrating and empowering the dispossessed poor, has in general made their situation worse precisely because it has been a crucial constitutive process in the creation of the post-industrial social order as it is lived by people in post-industrial cities. Exclusive development is meant to exclude after all.

This chapter examines the actual forms of socio-spatial division and the development of those forms in contemporary post-industrial societies. As before, this examination includes consideration of the significance of class, gender and age. Here we shall have to think of class not only as some kind of unidimensional attribute derived from income or occupation, or even as some kind of compound derived from both, but instead as something which is, even as an attribute, expressed through spatial residence itself.

We need to consider, not just nominalist attributes, but the reality of emergent social forms which are spatial in character. Spatial concentration of levels in the social hierarchy generates spatially distinctive cultural forms, especially when spatial concentration means that there is little social contact among the levels of the social order. If 'cultures of poverty' do exist, spatial concentration is a key element in their generation.[1]

We shall explore the social implications of spatial concentration through a consideration of the idea of 'community' (a term which for reasons which will become apparent will always be in inverted commas in this chapter), in the cities of post-industrial metropolitan capitalism. 'Community' matters not just because it is the key collective identity constituted through space, but also because 'community' development has been just about the only strategy of empowerment attempted, however half-heartedly and sometime with a view to disempowerment rather than empowerment, in the whole repertoire of anti-exclusion policy.

Having described space, and the dynamics of space in terms of the contrary but intimately associated processes of gentrification and residualization, we shall examine the very limited evidence available on the actual micro dynamics of people and households within space. In this examination we shall pay particular attention to the ways in which people use spatial relocation as a way of accessing collective consumption which is crucial for their own and their children's future life courses and to the related significance of space as consumption badge. We shall also consider the very far from trivial significance of space as immediate determinant of employment opportunities.

Finally the chapter reviews the constitutive role of social policies in the creation of excluding and dispossessing space. Attention is paid to the potential effectiveness and likely outcome of 'inclusionary' policies which are spatial either in the sense that they are about the uses of space as determined through urban planning or in that they are targeted on particular spatially defined populations. Some combine both approaches. Of particular significance here will be the idea of 'partnership' as a means for the reintegration of excluded 'communities'.

Divided cities: the reality

Danson and Mooney (1998: 232–3) make some important cautionary points about conventional static descriptions of 'dual cities' but dynamic quantitative ecology shows us that cities are becoming polarized spaces.[2] I really know of only two sets of studies which have used numerical taxonomy for dynamic exploration over time in particular cities. One is my own examinations of northern Tyneside and Teesside (see Byrne and Parson 1983; Byrne 1989a, 1995). The other is an examination of the classical locus of urban social ecology, Chicago, by Morenoff and Tienda (1997). They found considerable social polarization understood as a process which happens over time. In particular, transitional working-class neighbourhoods, which comprised 45 per cent of all census tracts in 1970, formed only 14 per cent of such tracts in 1990 (Morenoff and Tienda 1997: 67). Hispanic immigration had modified the social ecology of Chicago with concentration of Hispanics leading to the transition of many stable middle-class neighbourhoods to the transitional working-class category. In Chicago 'underclass' neighbourhoods were overwhelmingly (90 per cent on average) black.

Much of the scepticism about the idea of 'dual cities' has come from a largely justified critique of the oversimplistic application of the idea to 'world cities' (see Hamnett 1994). However, actual narratives of the history of socio-spatial systems over the transition to post-industrialism, whether quantitative or qualitative or both, across almost all advanced industrial cities whatever the 'welfare regime' within which they are embedded, demonstrate social polarization. As Fainstein and Harloe (1992) note in their comparison of London and New York: 'similar economic processes have been accompanied by similar socio-spatial outcomes despite quite different political and institutional traditions' (1992: 2). We find this in British industrial cities, in Dublin (see Byrne 1984; Bartley 1998), Paris (Wacquant 1993), Chicago, New York, London and in Poland, in Katowice and Lodz (Byrne and Wodz 1997; Grolowska-Leder and Warzywoda-Kruszynska 1997). Fainstein *et al.* (1992) remarked that

> If the concept of a 'dual' or 'polarizing' city is of any real utility, it can serve only as a hypothesis, the prelude to empirical analysis, rather than as a conclusion which takes the existence of confirmatory evidence for granted.
>
> (Fainstein *et al.* 1992: 13)

The evidence is now overwhelming. It does not show that all post-industrial cities are polarized. It shows that they are polarizing, and that those which are fully subject to liberalizing post-industrial capitalism are polarized.

Hamnett (1996) has argued very forcibly that to see socio-spatial polarization as an inevitable consequence of economic restructuring is to neglect the significance of different welfare regimes. Madanipour *et al.* (1998) argue on the same lines:

> Urban socio-spatial structures vary. In some social exclusion and spatial segregation are virtually synonymous. Others exhibit a more fine-grained pattern of differentiation. In some places, ethnicity and race form fundamental dividing lines in socio-spatial structures. In other places, culture and kinship networks are more significant. Finally, specific patterns of local governance and welfare state provision affect local patterns of social exclusion.
>
> (Madanipour *et al.* 1998: 8–9)

This ought to be true, but the reality is that existing variation seems to be much more a function of the different rates of progression of flexible globalization than of anything else, the point Gorzelak (1996) has made so pertinently about the future of the post-communist states of central Europe. This is at least as much a matter of ideological hegemony as of inevitable systemic tendency. It is a consequence of policy choices as these interact with market forces. Actors make it happen but actors in different places are acting in the same way.

Race/ethnicity and exclusion through space

There seems to be only one uniquely national element in socio-spatial exclusion in metropolitan capitalism. This is the ghettoization of black citizens in the USA, generated by the racism derived from the history of chattel slavery and the continuing reality of ethnic segregation to a unique and intense degree of black from white Americans. Massey and Denton (1993) define the situation in these terms: 'racial residential segregation is the principal structural feature of American society responsible for the perpetuation of urban poverty and represents a primary cause of racial inequality in the US'. They go on:

> black segregation is not comparable to the limited and transient segregation experienced by other racial and ethnic groups, now or in the past. No group in the history of the US has ever experienced the high level of residential segregation that has been imposed on blacks in large American cities in the past fifty years. This extensive racial isolation did not just happen; it was manufactured by whites through a series of self-conscious actions and purposeful institutional arrangements that continue today. Not only is the depth of black segregation unprecedented and utterly unique compared with that of other groups, but it shows little sign of change with the passage of time or improvement in socio-economic status.
>
> (Massey and Denton 1993: 2)

Wacquant's (1993) comparison of the black American ghetto and the French urban periphery illustrates the uniqueness of the US situation very well. He notes that:

> the colour line of which the black ghetto is the most visible institutional expression is so ingrained in the make up of the American urban landscape that it has become part of the order of things: racial division is a thoroughly taken for granted constituent of the organization of the metropolitan economy, society and polity . . . the French banlieue remains a heterogeneous universe in which racial or ethnic categories have little social potency.
>
> (Wacquant 1993: 373–5)

In metropolitan capitalism the French situation is the norm. If anything evidence from the UK shows that with two significant exceptions the saliency of race/ethnicity is even less than in France. The British evidence comes from the series of studies carried out on the small area data available from the 1991 Census. These show that there are series of ethnicities with very different social relations surrounding them. Indeed those who identify as black are the least separated from the UK white population as Peach (1996: 23) indicates in the passage quoted on pp. 91–2.

At the socio-spatial level the important point is that with the exception of the situation of Bangladeshis in the East End of London and Catholics in working class urban Northern Ireland, there is no evidence of the existence of constrained ghettos (see Peach 1996). 'Black' British and Afro-Caribbean people are found in all social locations in UK cities, although they may have areas of relative concentration. People of South Asian origin are (with the exception of constrained Bangladeshi estates in East London) less likely to live in social housing, where there is evidence of a pattern of racial hostility towards them. However, there is no evidence of racial exclusion from middle-class neighbourhoods. This is a contradictory situation. 'Other than White and other than Black' ethnic minorities are spatially excluded, but only from the residualized and excluded locales. This matters because spatial segregation is so crucial for general social exclusion. As Massey and Denton (1993) remark:

> Because of racial segregation, a significant share of black America is condemned to experience a social environment where poverty and joblessness are the norm, where most families are on welfare, where educational failure prevails, and where social and physical deterioration abound.
>
> (Massey and Denton 1993: 2)

The significance of spatial segregation for social exclusion in the UK is immense, but, other than in the North of Ireland and for East London Bangladeshis, the fundamental principle of this segregation is class, not ethnicity.

Rex (1973) argued that the 'other than White' ethnic minorities of the UK were likely to be the basis of a permanent racially distinctive underclass in the society. The evidence is that this is not the case in any simple sense. The 'Black' groups (other than the very rapidly growing recent Black African immigration, much of which comes as middle class) are assimilating into the white working class through intermarriage and common residence. This is usually described as the 'Irish' route. Indians, Chinese and Black Africans seem to be following an education/business route usually described in the UK literature as 'Jewish' towards assimilation into the middle class, although there remains a very significant Indian working class. The use of the terms 'Irish' and 'Jewish' routes is, as Chance (1997: 237) observes, 'particularly ironic, because little is known about the Irish, far less is known about the Jewish population in Britain'. The Pakistani and Bangladeshi populations, defined perhaps in common by their adherence to Indian subcontinent versions of combinations of Islam and tradition (which are of particular significance for that large part of the Pakistani population originating from Mirpur in Azad Kashmir), do seem to be much more excluded in terms of overall characteristics. However, significant though these groups are, they are not large enough to form any kind of real overall reserve army.

Poland, since the Holocaust and Stalin's reconstruction of European geography, is on the face of things an ethnically homogeneous society in which more than 97 per cent of the people are Polish Catholics. However, there are some quasi-ethnic differences, the most interesting of which is the distinction in Upper Silesia between autochthonous Silesians and post-Second World War immigrants from elsewhere in Poland. Both groups are Slav and Catholic and have historically asserted a Polish national identity. However, in a series of studies Wodz (1994a) shows that the segregation of autochthonous Silesians in older workers' settlements, the *familioks*, and the very strong commitment of Silesians to a highly proletarianized culture of heavy industrial employment, may lead to this group being particularly disadvantaged by the processes of deindustrialization. These are exceptionally severe in this most industrialized of all central European regions (Wodz 1994b). She places very considerable emphasis on the socio-spatial differentiation of the Katowice conurbation, which is in large part an almost accidental product of the phases of industrialization. Certainly the intensely proletarianized autochthonous Silesians, who together with their near neighbours, the Czech and East German working classes, are really the only groups to have experienced both capitalist and Soviet industrialization, are 'ripe' for dispossession. This process is already underway through coal mine closure.

Gender and exclusion through space

There is a considerable and interesting literature on gender and space but it seldom deals with the role of gender as a principle for segregation in residential space. Given the continuing predominance of heterosexual couples as the bases of households, gender segregation in residence is essentially a function of the spatial segregation of female headed single parent households.

In the United States examinations of the phenomenon are inextricably bound up with considerations of different familial patterns by ethnic group. However, in the UK ethnicity is not the principle concomitant of single parenthood. On the contrary since the late 1970s there has been a massive increase in single parenthood, particularly among the overwhelmingly dominant autochthonous white UK population. In 1971 8 per cent of families with children were headed by a lone parent. By 1994, 23 per cent of families with children were headed by a lone parent (Rowlingson and McKay 1998: 3).

Socio-spatial studies of divided cities show very clearly that while there is by no means an absolute segregation of lone parent headed households, such households form a much larger proportion of all households with dependent children in the poorer halves of divided cities than they do in the affluent halves. For example in 1991 in Cleveland and Leicester the proportions of all households headed by lone parents in the poorer halves of those urban areas were 28 per cent and 29 per cent respectively. In the affluent halves of both cities the equivalent figure was 7 per cent in both cases (Byrne 1997a: 62). All socio-spatial classifications of urban areas in the UK reveal a similar pattern.

The origins of this pattern lie in the way in which households gain access to housing. The very real financial advantages which attach to the owner occupation of dwellings means that since the early 1960s UK households which can afford to buy their own homes have generally sought to do so. This does not mean that all owner occupiers live in the better halves of cities. The tenure is now so dominant that it contains a wide variety of housing including some formerly privately rented older stock in the poorer half of divided cities.

The spatial segregation of single parent headed households derives from their relative concentration outwith the owner-occupied housing stock and within social housing rented from local authorities or housing associations. Whereas three-quarters of couple households are owner occupiers, this is the case for less than one-third of single parents (Ford and Miller 1998b: 16). This concentration results from the poverty of single parents who are not excluded from access to social housing by low income but cannot afford to buy. It also reflects the dynamics of social housing in the UK over the 80-year lifetime of this tenure as a significant part of the general housing stock.

Social housing on a mass scale was originally built for the respectable working class, not for the poor. Indeed the most important differentiation which operated in relation to it, right up until the 1970s, was not between it and other tenures but within it between those estates built under slum clearance legislation for the poor and those built to deal with general housing needs, usually to a much higher quality, which were a key location of the central working class (see Merrett 1979). This has changed since 1979. First, much of the best social housing has been sold off into owner occupation through tenant purchase. Second, new couple households with reasonable incomes have considerable financial and social incentives to purchase housing rather than rent it. The result is that much of the family housing stock, particularly in cities other than London, is now occupied by a mix of elderly people continuing to live in the family home of their adult lives, people in couple households with low or no wages, and single parents.

Single parents in the UK and France, and to a more limited extent in the USA, can gain access to social housing stock because they have children, on a needs rather than resources basis. However, contrary to urban myth, this is not a process of young girls having babies to get houses or flats. Rowlingson and McKay (1998) show that this motive did not figure in the life stories of their respondents. We are actually looking far more at the fragility of couple households for the poor under post-industrial capitalism.

There is a very considerable dynamic movement between the household form based on the poor couple single parenthood. Single parents form new unions. Single parent households are formed by the break-up of couples. The significance of the enormous difference in marriage/cohabitation rates between the two halves of the divided cities is of great significance here. In the typical and reasonably prosperous UK city of Leicester, I found that in the poorer third of the city less than half of all registered births were registered by married parents, whereas in the more affluent two-thirds, more than 90 per cent of births were registered by married parents. Most births were registered by both parents but in the poorer parts of this divided city more births were registered by two parents who were not married than by two parents who were married.

It is conventional to comment on the strain imposed on couplehood by the insecurity and low level of male wages for unskilled workers, a vastly more significant challenge to the conventional family form than any change in the character of sexual morality. In the concentration of single parents in UK social housing we are seeing the result of three dynamic processes. First, and quantitatively the least significant, we see the consequence of the housing of poor young benefit-dependent, never-married mothers. Second, we see the consequence of the downwards drift of divorcees from couple households in owner occupation who have lost their owner-occupied dwelling on divorce for financial reasons. Third, we see the ongoing dynamic movement from couple to single to couple to single and so on by households. This is in aggregate a function of the wage and labour relations of the dispossessed poor, whatever the contingent circumstances relating to each individual household dissolution or formation.

Age and social exclusion through space

Now I want to examine the spatial significance of age separations, or more precisely to consider the position of young people. Let me quote from Wacquant (1993) whose observation about the Parisian suburbs echoes absolutely in relation to my own considerable – (25 years plus) experience as community worker and inner city councillor in the North East of England:[3]

If there is a dominant antagonism which runs through the Red Belt cité and stamps the collective consciousness of its inhabitants, it is not, contrary to widespread media representations, one that opposes immigrants (especially 'Arabs') and autochthonous French families but the cleavage dividing youth (les jeunes), native and foreign lumped together, for all other social categories. Youths are widely singled out by older residents as the chief source of vandalism, delinquency and insecurity, and they are publicly held up as responsible for worsening condition, and reputation of the degraded banlieue.

(Wacquant 1993: 376)

Traditionally these criticisms have been directed against male youths, but young women do also figure. They are less involved in street display, but are by no means not involved. What causes difficulties in UK social housing is the behaviour of a minority of young, never-married, female single parents whose dwellings become the base for rowdy parties and publicly displayed sexual behaviour. In some cases such young women operate under considerable male coercion but this is by no means invariable. In my experience, participant observation, as an inner city councillor, I found no hostility by older residents to single parents as such. Residents were perfectly aware of the dynamics of both tenure and household form. What they wanted was neighbours who did not create public disturbances.[4]

In his examination of Red Belt *cités* Wacquant reiterates a point made by Damer (1989) in an earlier study. We are seriously in error if we treat locales like Glasgow's Wine Alley as internally undifferentiated. For those who live there they are micro socio-spatial systems with a complex internal structure. It is the outward labelling that matters in relation to overall social location and social exclusion. Let us now consider the nature of social relations in the spaces of dispossession.

'Communities'?

residents of the French cité and the American ghetto each from an *impossible community*, perpetually divided against themselves, which cannot but refuse to acknowledge the collective nature of their predicament and who are therefore inclined to deploy strategies of distancing and 'exit' that tend to validate negative outside perceptions and feed a deadly self-fulfilling prophecy through which public taint and collective disgrace eventually produce that which they claim merely to record: namely social atomism, community 'disorganization' and cultural anomie.

(Wacquant 1993: 374, original emphasis)

In this section I want to examine the emergent social forms which derive from the common residence of people in excluded space. There are two terms which are used in discussing these, terms which are different but have a considerable degree of intersection. These are 'community' and 'culture'. 'Community' is a tricky word in every sense. Crowe and Allan (1994) note that although the term originally had a clear spatial referent, it is now being used to identify 'communities of interest' without a spatial basis. To my mind one of the most useful definitions was that given in 1944 by Glass when she distinguished between neighbourhoods which were simply people living in an area and experiencing the same things, from 'communities' which were conscious of the communality which derived from common spatial experience and were willing to act communally. The parallel with Marx's distinction between class in and for itself is clear. Here we are dealing with spatial 'communities', although the identification of specific communities is much more likely to be a function of arbitrary dictat by administrative powers than to be the product of autonomous social action. At the same time Wacquant's account of the atomized nature of social relations in excluded spaces, an account which argues against the existence of a clear coherent collective identity of interest *and* action, rings absolutely true. A turn to a consideration of the nature of culture may help us to understand this contradiction.

The most recent exponent of the idea of an emergent cultural differentiation of the poor is Wilson (1992) although he explicitly disowns the term 'culture of poverty'. Wilson makes it clear that he is concerned with the 'ghetto poor' of the deindustrializing cities of the US frostbelt. This focusing is important. As Rose (1991) has pointed out, the Wilson (1992) thesis relates the micro level of neighbourhood to the macro level of economic forces through asserting that conditions in the one are a result of changes in the other (Rose 1991: 491–2). For Wilson the primary causal process is deindustrialization but he argues that this may create social situations through spatial segregation, which lead to the reproduction of a new cultural order. Hence Wilson's concern about the single parent headed family and the absence of successful, middle class, black role models. In essence Wilson sees the social atomization described by Wacquant as part of a cultural form. We might go further by employing a specifically dynamic view and see the antagonism between youth and elders as representing an emergent tendency with the youth attitudes being at least the basis of the new culture. Note that the emergent culture is not constructed around spatially ordered solidarities. It is highly individualistic and self-centred.

We must recognize that Wilson and Wacqant's accounts of atomization are very different both from reactionary 'Calvinistic' blaming of the poor and from the rather optimistic original version of the culture of poverty proposed by the personally radical Lewis (1966). Harvey and Reed (1996) argue that:

> the virtue of Lewis' thesis lies in the clarity with which it demonstrates that poverty's subculture is not a mere 'tangle of pathology', but consists, instead, of a set of *positive adaptive mechanisms*. These adaptive

mechanisms are socially constructed, that is, collectively fabricated by the poor from the substance of their everyday lives, and they allow the poor to survive in otherwise impossible material and social conditions . . . Unlike other explanations of poverty, it concedes that the poor have been damaged by the system but insists that this damage does not disqualify them from determining their own fate. This last judgement is something many social scientists of both the left and right have forgotten.

(Harvey and Reed 1996: 466, original emphasis)

This is an important point, especially when associated with Reed and Harvey's (1992) insistence on the development of a class-based politics of poverty. Both Reed and Harvey's and Wilson's accounts are class analyses. Wilson has asserted strongly, and in my view appropriately, that he writes as a social democrat. However, his account is one of absolute disempowerment, of disintegration under the conditions of externally mediated industrial restructuring, and of a social restructuring towards individualistic and anomic decollectivized response to the impacts of such changes. There is a thesis of culture, but of disabling culture as a product of basal change. My own account of Teesside (Byrne 1995) is broadly similar, as is Wacquant's (1993) of Chicago and Paris.

In contrast Reed and Harvey (1996), after Lewis (1966), assert that the separate social identity of the poor can be a resource for collective action. Lewis's own work provides good evidence for this, although Harvey's (1993) fascinating study of white poverty in the US mid-West describes collective strategies for survival rather than transformation. However, the point is important. Difference is not always disadvantageous. There is a complex argument here which hinges around the articulation of social and economic relations between the poor/excluded and the 'core' working class (although as Reed and Harvey note in an era of flexible employment, that status is contingent for many of us). Here, we need to note that collective situation when recognized as such can be the basis of constructive collective action and equally note that such a situation will produce collectivity only if there is some degree of personal permanence in it.

Let me summarize this complicated but important argument. There are three versions of the cultural position of the poor. The first is that of those who blame the poor for their poverty. Even when, as with Glazer and Moynihan in the USA in the 1960s (see Harvey 1993 and Lemann 1991), there is a recognition of the historical construction of different social practices, the poor are blamed for their continued participation in this deviance. This argument holds little water in relation to, for example, the massive growth in non-marital parenthood in the UK. This fits exactly with the second account, essentially Wilson's (1987) account, in which the combined effects of deindustrialization and socio-spatial segregation have engendered a new, atomized and disorganized deviant culture which exists because the poor are constrained into such a cultural form. For Lewis (1966) and for Reed and Harvey (1996) the cultural forms of the poor are certainly a product of structural social relations which exclude and dispossess them, but they may represent a real resource for future social action. Freire (1977) would certainly agree with that proposition, and it will serve us here as a note towards the conclusion of this text.

Traditional discussions of 'community' always emphasize not merely shared space but continued and long term temporal stability. 'Communities' are made up of people who live together for a long time. I am actually deeply suspicious of the notion of absolute temporal stability even in the most remote rural locations. I am absolutely certain that urban 'communities' have a very high degree of spatial mobility into and out of them and always have had. What are the spatial dynamics of people in urban space in the post-industrial city? There are actually no micro studies I am aware of that actually document such mobility in detail. The British Household Panel Study is relatively useless in terms of spatial data and I have not seen any studies from its US equivalent which chart movement around the elements of specific local socio-spatial systems. What we do have are some gross aggregate data descriptions of movement derived from administrative records, census data and some ad-hoc studies.

In Cramlington, on the outskirts of Tyneside, in the late 1980s I found that the rates of household mobility from both 'difficult to let' estates and from ordinary owner-occupied areas were very high with annual turnovers in excess of 20 per cent (see Byrne 1989b). Plainly some households would stay put for a long time but many moved. Indeed I found from administrative records that there was a quite substantial movement from ordinary areas into 'the difficult to let' estates which derived from both marital break-ups and job loss. Likewise there was some less good evidence of movement out of the 'difficult to let' estates back to owner occupation.[5]

There is a real need for studies of spatial movement through time. All the available impressionistic, anecdotal and (fairly minimal) flow studies suggest that this dynamic is an important part of people's life courses. Certainly one of the key problems of area centred 'inclusion' policies which focus on the changing of individuals, usually through some programme of training, is that in atomized and anomic locales such people use the wages which training may bring them to get out.

This relates rather closely to one of the commonest observations made by residents of deprived and dispossesses spaces in describing their relations with the labour market. Wacquant's respondents in the Parisian *banlieues* (suburbs) and the Chicago projects and residents of the Meadowell in North Tyneside and other UK 'outer estates' all assert that residence as signified by address operates as a basis for discrimination against them when they are seeking employment. They are badged by the space they occupy. Note that this is an aspect which has particular significance in relation to formal labour markets and relatively privileged positions in the contemporary division of labour. Residence badges and that matters a good deal as a basis for excluding closure.

Making excluding space: the role of social policies

There are three sets of policies which have the effect of promoting exclusion through space. The first are those policies which, while not in any way spatial in inherent form, do have spatially differentiating consequences. Hamnett (1997) has written pertinently about the spatial impact of reduced higher levels of taxation in cancelling out the redistributive effects of regional policies. The same goes even more strongly in relation to intra-urban income distribution.

The second consists of those policies which provide social benefits on a spatial basis in a way which is differentiating and which affects future life chances. In summary these take the form of spatial distribution of public benefits around an existing socio-spatial system. By far the most important of these is the operation of public schooling systems. Massey and Denton (1993) and Bankston and Caldas (1996) have examined the enormous significance of ethnic segregation in the USA. Together with Rogers (Byrne and Rogers 1996) I examined the pattern of school success in relation to the social character of its spatially defined catchment area for England. The results of such studies all indicate that in general the character of schools reflects the character of the areas from which the children in them come. There are emergent properties (see Byrne 1998: Chapter 7) which derive from the interactions among children and socio-spatial location which have a profound effect on educational attainment. This matters a great deal, both in terms of inherent effect and because it leads to an atomized and family only programme of action by people. They seek to get the best for their children, in the UK often by using 'parental choice' to insert their children into schools in 'better' areas (see Brown 1995; Byrne and Rogers 1996).

The third set of spatial policies which matter in relation to exclusion are those which actually constitute the form of socio-spatial systems. It is very important to remember that these cannot be understood simply as reactive to the general changes in the social order which have been described in terms of a transition from an industrial to post-industrial system. On the contrary they have played a crucial part in the constitution of that very social order.

Madanipour et al. (1998) note that we cannot understand the development of cities unless we understand the complex processes of public and private governance which manage the planning process. Here the words public and private must always be understood as containing a double meaning. They refer both the public and private as spheres, i.e. to government and to private capital. They also refer to the actual conduct of processes of determination, to the public mode of democracy and the 'private' mode of corporatism. In contemporary cities much of the process of governance of urban space is conducted in private in a corporatist mode. In the UK an effort has been made in City Challenge and in its successor 'Single Regeneration Budget' (see Geddes 1997) to include 'communities' in this process through incorporated representative, but Geddes (1997) shows that such 'community' participation is at best confined to matters of the management of details of implementation and never has an influence on strategy where global imperatives of development are taken as a given. These instances matter a great deal both in substantive content and because they show us the actual exclusion from power which is a crucial part of social exclusion as a general process. Eversley's (1990) bitter condemnation of the direction of modern planning was exactly accurate. What we have seen with catalytic planning (see Byrne 1999) is the shaping of space to be unequal.

In general urban regeneration schemes, typified by the UK Urban Development Corporations (UDCs) (see Imrie and Thomas 1999), have been primarily about the regeneration of land. Indeed in the UDC programme social development was specifically dismissed as an actual objective of policy. At best benefits were to trickle down. The story of the impact of 'growth coalitions' on US cities, including the archetype of Baltimore, is exactly similar. Fitch's (1993) *The Assassination of New York* explains the current state of the city in terms of the planning ideologies, interests and actions of the 'Finance, Insurance and Real Estate' (FIRE) elite who have dominated its planning processes. For Fitch 'post-industrial' New York is a 'mutation masquerading as a modernization . . . a "Throwback"' (Fitch 1993: 235) to the pre-industrial archaic urban form in which the city belonged to the elite consumers dominating and exploiting the producers placed outside it and somewhere else. Fitch's book is exactly and explicitly a history of agency, of active deindustrialization as a programme carried out by a coherent and identifiable elite. It is a story of actors.

In the UK, City Challenge and Single Regeneration Budget schemes (which followed UDCs) have incorporated both social objectives in terms of employment and housing, and a degree of public participation, precisely because the UDC programme had become identified both with private capital rooking the public purse for massive subsidies and with the absolute disregard of the interests of inner-city working-class 'communities'. The shift to partnership was supposed to redress the balance but Geddes (1997) demonstrates that the benefits of partnership in terms of both outcome and process seem to have been minimal.

This is not simply because the interests of development capital have been given absolute priority. That has been possible only because in 'partnership' there has been no real countervailing power from the 'community' precisely because the 'community' is so fragmented and disorganized. Given the fragmented nature of 'community' and the logic of personal mobility in space, the proposals contained in the Cabinet Office Social Exclusion Unit 1998 White Paper *Bringing Britain Together: A National Strategy for Neighbourhood Renewal* (Cm 4045) can be described only as vacuous. The authors of this piece seem simply not to know how people actually conduct their lives in the divided city. It is plain that organization is the key to any kind of re-empowerment of the dispossessed. That is the issue to which we now turn in the conclusion to this book. It is process which matters most when we are dealing with issues of power.

Conclusion

The conclusion to this chapter cannot be optimistic. The creation of the post-industrial city through the combined and interacting effects of the global reorganization of capitalist production and the pursuit of fragmenting urban policy, has disempowered the organized working class of advanced capitalism in the sphere of reproduction. This disempowerment has many aspects, but it is particularly significant in terms of the fragmentation of 'community'. The history of working-class politics of reproduction, a history much more 'hidden' than that of the working class at the point of production, is a history of action founded in the solidarities which emerged from common residence in the spaces of cities. This was of course to a considerable extent a politics carried out by women, which perhaps explains its neglect in formal history.

Wacquant's (1993) account of the way in which those spaces are now much less spaces of solidarity is accurate and extremely important. Crucial to that weakening of solidarity is the actual micro dynamics of personal lives. People do not act with their neighbours. In the post-industrial city they act to leave their neighbours – to move to spaces of relative comfort and security. The spatial divides of exclusion are the most evident and real expression of the social division of post-industrial capitalism. They are the product of the dynamics of capitalist restructuring at the macro level. They are disempowered by the dynamics of personal strategies in the divided cities which that restructuring has engendered. Can things be made different?

Conclusion: what is and what
is to be done about it

The conclusion to this book has two purposes. First, and briefly, it presents a summary account of the nature of social exclusion based on the ideas and data reviewed up to this point. Second, it examines what we might do about social exclusion, assuming that we want to do anything. That examination is in turn divided into two sections. It begins with a consideration of the nature of the politics of social inclusion, with a review of just what political identities might contribute to the restoration of a social world of advanced capitalism which is at least as inclusive as Fordism was, and might even go beyond this both in terms of the internal degree of inclusion and of the extension of that inclusion on a global scale. The term 'political identity' is used here really as a kind of label for political collectives defined by both common objectives and common principles as the joint bases for action. It includes consciousness, but goes beyond it. It is not just about material interest, but about ideas that collectivities of people have about what the future should be and why that future should be.

The second part of the 'what is to be done' section of this conclusion focuses on the possibilities for organization of the 'excluded'. It considers the possibility of conscientizing community development, of a practical pedagogy of the dispossessed and those who are not dispossessed but have a common material and moral interest with the dispossessed. Both sections will make demands, particularly upon the Christian churches, as well as on Social Democratic, Christian Democratic and Green political movements. The demands on the churches should be couched particularly aggressively. The Christian churches know what is going on. They have seen – they have begun to judge. It is well time they acted.[1]

The excluded many, the 'at risk' most, and the excluding few

The crucial element for any understanding of the nature and implication of social exclusion is a grasp of the significance of the real dynamics of social life under post-industrial capitalism. These dynamics are very different from those of Fordism. Indeed they are probably different from the dynamics of advanced capitalist societies at any time between the 1860s and the 1970s. Throughout that period in general, most people in advanced capitalist societies had better lives than their own parents. This is immediately obvious for the very large numbers who were immigrants into the industrial world from peasant peripheries, but it was true generation upon generation for those born into industrial society as well.

Not only was there a continuing rise in real living standards, but also throughout this period there was a very considerable degree of upward social mobility associated with expansion in the proportion of more desirable occupational roles. Social mobility seemed to be a real possibility, with much of that mobility derived from the acquisition of better educational qualifications.

During the golden years of Keynesianism, the combination of full employment and strong trade unions with a considerable growth in household earnings, derived in large part from increased economic participation by married women, meant that most households could reasonably access a material standard of living which was that of the general social norm. For example, most council housing estates in the UK were occupied by working class people with steady jobs and a standard of living broadly comparable with that of those living in owner-occupied areas. Movement from council housing to owner occupation was often the product of quite small incremental gains in income.[2]

Upward social mobility was very general. When Banim (1986) surveyed the residents of a desirable middle income owner-occupied estate at Chapel Park in Newcastle, she found that the overwhelming majority were the children of manual worker households and had been brought up in council housing or privately rented accommodation. They had achieved upward mobility in space often through a simple combination of a skilled male worker's earnings and those of a clerical female employee. This mobility was absolutely dependent on the availability of well paid male manual employment.

The point is that the real personal dynamics of Fordist industrial capitalism were dynamics of degree. There were very poor people living in appalling conditions in the industrial cities but for most people the middle range of experience was the norm and most people saw a prospect of upward mobility for themselves or their children. Crucially throughout this period the incomes of those in the bottom half of the income distribution improved relative to those in the top 10 per cent of that distribution.

The dynamics of personal mobility are very different now, particularly in intergenerational terms. We now find a situation in which upward educational mobility in terms of acquisition of educational qualifications can be associated with downward social mobility in terms of income. There are very many graduates now who earn less in the USA and the UK than their skilled manual worker fathers used to earn, in the USA in real terms and in the UK in relative terms. The skilled manual jobs are now not available of course, and this is even more true for the semi-skilled jobs where high earnings were dependent on union power. Note that there are many young women graduates in the new clerical employment who earn no more relatively and often less than their factory worker mothers or grandmothers earned under Fordism. They are certainly less powerful as part of a collectivity. The panoptical surveying of call centre workers contrasts vividly with the union based capacity of female printing or clothing workers in the late 1960s. Above all the relative security of employment, not necessarily but often with the same employer, has gone. It was never so much a matter under Fordism of a 'job for life' as a job always available somewhere.

So what then is 'social exclusion' in post-industrial capitalism? The answer usually given to that question involves examination of the lives of people in the bottom third of the income distribution. It cannot be constructed around income alone, precisely because both the form of the income distribution taken as a snapshot and consideration of the dynamics of household incomes show that there is no easy boundary to be drawn in income terms. Townsend's (1979) efforts to construct an index of social participation and establish a qualitative change in this in relation to the passing of an income threshold are meaningful only in snapshot terms. They would apply if conditions through time were relatively permanent, but if there is a high level of income dynamism they cannot be generalized.

If we turn to descriptions of condition as opposed to income, we are little further forward. Social exclusion is often equated with permanent unemployment, but the reality is that permanent unemployment is a relatively uncommon condition in contrast with the phenomenon of *chômage d'exclusion*, the cycling from unemployment to poorly paid work, whether within the regular economy or the irregular economy, and back, with an equal cycling between full dependency on state benefits and dependency on Speenhamland supplements to low incomes. For the young there is an additional device on this merry-go-round – experience of 'training'. The issue here is not low income taken alone, but the combination of low income and insecurity of employment. Insecurity of employment is inherent in a flexible labour market.

It is much easier to identify 'excluded (and excluding) spaces', the consequence of the transition of cities to a post-industrial status, a transition which of course is as much the product of policy as of inherent shifts in capitalist production and reproduction. Here taxonomic procedures do generate a sharp and clear divide which corresponds exactly with popular conceptions. However, we have to remember that people move in space as well as through time. Those who live in the peripheral estates of the Red Belt of Paris or the outer estates of Glasgow or Sunderland in the UK are clearly living in excluded spaces, but the degree of movement into and out of these places is very considerable. This is extremely important when we come to consider the bases of community action.

In general, public policy in Europe, and even more in the USA, sees social exclusion in the weak sense as defined by Veit-Wilson (1998). The excluded are marked by personal deficits. Their exclusion can be remedied by the correction of those personal deficits. The argument of this book is that exclusion is not a property of individuals or even of social spaces. Rather it is a necessary and inherent characteristic of an unequal post-industrial capitalism founded around a flexible labour market and with a systematic constraining of the organizational powers of workers as collective actors.

Social exclusion programmes predominantly centre on the rectification of personal deficits through training. They are founded on a supply side notion: if only these people could acquire the skills which the higher levels of the labour market want of them, then everything would be fine. They would be taken up by business in reasonably paid work. The only programmes which do not take this form are the Clinton administration's tax credit schemes and the closely related provisions of the 1998 UK Budget. The absolute foundation of these 'innovative' programmes is exactly the same as that of the Speenhamland system. US President Clinton and UK Chancellor Brown have come to the same conclusion as the Berkshire magistrates did in the 1790s. The post-industrial system now can no more generate a living wage for all necessary workers than the agricultural system could then. There is, however, one very substantial difference. The Berkshire magistrates taxed the capitalist farmers through the poor rate. Transfers were vertical. The contemporary versions of Speenhamland tax other workers with slightly higher wages. Transfers are essentially horizontal. It is very important to recognize the analytical account which underpins these tax credit policies which are the product of two of what were the great organizational supporters of the Keynes/Beveridge approach to governance, the US Democrats and UK Labour. Policies founded around wage supplements involve an absolute acceptance of the immutability of the market reward system of an unequal capitalism.

If we use the language of chaos/complexity to describe the contemporary social order of post-industrial capitalism and the actual trajectories of individuals and households within it, then we can see that contemporary social policies accept a world in which there are quite distinctive ensembles of trajectories. There are multiple attractors and these are taken as given. Basically there are three attractor states. First, there is that of being excluded which is most easily badged in a univariate nominalist way by residence in excluded space, but which comprises a set of life course trajectories revolving around movement among poor work and benefit dependency. Then there is the domain of 'insecurity'. Here people have work and a general standard of living which approximates to that normal under Fordism, but with personal situation being massively less secure than it was in that period.

It is very important to note that there is considerable personal and inter-generational mobility between these two condition sets. That is demonstrated absolutely by the information we have about income and employment dynamics and the limited information we have about residential dynamics. Social exclusion policies as they exist at present are all about moving people from the excluded to the merely contingent domains. They seek to do this through either or both of training/education and the supplementation of low wages.

The third attractor set is that of the affluent, the owners of capital and the higher service classes. This category is not closed. It can be entered, particularly through very high levels of educational attainment. These can of course be purchased. Perhaps some readers of this book are paying for the private secondary education of their own children, or at the very least arranging their area of residence so that their children have access to those state secondary schools with outstandingly good results in competitive examinations. However, it is perfectly evident that the possession of some combination of cultural and financial resources is the basis of membership of the superclass. In income terms this comprises the top 5 per cent of income recipients who are the beneficiaries of cuts in the higher rates of taxation and who have accumulated massive real wealth. We should also note that this superclass generally regards itself, in atheistic terms, as a Calvinist elect. Its members have 'achieved' through inherent worth and regard themselves as fully entitled to their consequent differentiating privileges.

Let us be absolutely clear here. So long as a social system exists which can be described in the terms just employed, then we will have social exclusion. What, if anything, can we do about it?

Can we do nothing? Is politics powerless?

Let me quote the summary of conclusions of the MOST Roskilde symposium 'From social exclusion to social cohesion: a policy agenda' held in advance of the United Nations Copenhagen World Summit on Social Development:

> Sixto Roxas . . . feels that since the nineteenth century Western civil-isation has made the market and its self-regulating capacity the basis for democracy, the liberal state itself being the creation of this market. The key to this system, which was at one time called into question with the development of the Keynesian welfare state, resides in the assertion that the laws which govern the market are of the same order as the universal laws of physics. It is therefore to be understood that a major characteristic of dominant economic thinking is that it considers itself to be scientifically based and universally valid. This gives it, in the words of Ignacy Sachs 'an ahistoric and atopic character'. One must attempt to understand, says Roxas, why the market has progressively

occupied the totality of the economic terrain and how economic theory has been able to transform itself into a dominant ideology. Such is the case today. Thanks to a powerful network structured by international financial institutions, and those issuing from Bretton Woods in particular, the dominant economic order is in the process of establishing a global hegemony of such omnipotence that one may truly speak of our epoch as the civilisation of the market, or of enterprise . . . The result of such an evolution is that, in Petrella's words, competitiveness 'is not longer a means; it has become the prime objective not just of enterprises but also of the state and society as a whole.' . . . Petrella agrees with Roxas in asserting that private enterprise is in the process of shaping the values of our times by fixing the rules of the game, not only for itself but also for the state and the whole of society. The constraint of the dominant economism is now such that states are enjoined to run themselves like private firms, whereas the latter take on an increasing number of prerogatives that were once in the exclusive domain of the state.

(Bessis 1995: 17–18)

This is absolutely accurate. If we examine the arguments of the report of Labour's Commission on Social Justice (Borrie 1994) we find that it distinguishes between a political line that it endorses, which it describes in terms of a political category of 'investors', and the old political objective of equality, which it dismissively associates with 'levellers'. Well, there is an honourable and acceptable label! I will bear the name leveller any time. What matters, however, is what Borrie meant by 'investors'. Simply put, these are those who have bought the ideological line that there is no alternative to the endorsement of the logic of market capitalism and that the only way in which to achieve social justice is to fit people for the purposes which market capitalism wants of them. Unlike Brown and Clinton, the members of the Commission believed that everybody could be moved by training and employment experience into the middle of the attractor sets described above. There was no notion that one of the roles of politics is to change the system to something different.

If social exclusion is inherent in a market-oriented flexible post-industrial capitalism, then it is impossible to eliminate it by any set of social policies directed at the excluded alone. It is perfectly true that redistribution through tax credits will benefit the working poor and that this has the enormous advantage for order of making poor work more economically rational for the working poor. However, this will be done entirely at the expense of the working non-poor, not at the expense of the beneficiaries of flexible post-industrial capitalism among the most affluent. Nelson (1995) has described the political context of policies of this sort:

the resources associated with post-industrial capitalism contribute to a more hegemonic political structure favoring business interests and wealthier individuals . . . This hegemonic structure erodes class conflict under post-industrial capitalism. Unions decline in importance, working-class politics recedes, and a conservative consensus becomes ever more embracing and pervasive. Hence the paradox of politics and class conflict under post-industrial capitalism: As inequality increases, the potential for militant conflict diminishes among those most affected by economic adversity and circumstance.

(Nelson 1995: 104)

We must recognize that certain sorts of interests are favoured in this process and others are excluded. Note the comments of an astute *Observer* journalist on who has influence in contemporary UK politics:

> The trades unions must rank as the lousiest investors in political influence. They have forked out more than £100 million on the Labour Party since 1979 . . . When finally they do get a Labour Government it does nothing more for unions than it would have done anyway and probably less. . . . [Blair] treats union leaders as if they are the carriers of an infectious disease. He deliberately bites the hand that feeds his party.

(Andrew Rawnsley, *Observer* 19 April 1998: 23)

These accounts are very similar to Jessop's (1994) 'hollowed out state' as outlined in Chapter 3 but there is a crucial distinction. Roxas and Petrella (see Bessis) recognize that the issue is to a very considerable degree one of ideological contestation, an important element in which is the assertion by the proponents of flexible post-industrial capitalism, that their future is the only future possible. Therborn (see Chapter 2) has noted the weakness of European Christian and Social Democratic politics in the face of this onslaught and we have to recognize that Anglo-American Keynesian politics, if not necessarily economic theory, has essentially ceded both the intellectual and the administrative ground to it. Solidarity is on the retreat and full employment has been ceded absolutely. This is how it is. How might it be made differently.

I was about to stop this section with that question. I cannot resist quoting from the headlines of this morning's *Guardian* (28 August 1998): 'Panic grips global markets – shock waves reach West – UK's growth "almost at zero"' and from the absolutely pertinent comment of L. Elliott in the body of the paper:

> Unfettered capitalism has done what Stalin could never do: It has brought the West to the brink of economic turmoil. Belatedly, it is now recognized that the financial and political crisis engulfing Russia is not just a problem for Boris Yeltsin but a threat to the stability of the entire global economy . . . Let's start with some basics. The prevailing philosophy of the past quarter-century has been that there is no such thing as too much liberalisation . . . At first only rightwing politicians believed in the new dogma, but eventually politicians of the left – chastened by electoral defeat – started to recite the globalisation mantra

as well. According to the new orthodoxy, there was nothing that could be done to hold back the new global forces, even if parties of the left wanted to. Which, sad to say, not many of them did by the mid-1990s.

(*Guardian* 28 August 1998: 16)

Amen to that! So we have not only a genuine crisis of capitalism but also a crisis of political will and identity. Can anything be done?

A solidaristic politics: agents and methods

The intellectual contest in terms of political ideas is important, but it is useless without actual practical engagement, without the redevelopment of a popular democratic politics of solidarity. How is that to be achieved? The first thing to do is to identify just what social forces might already have a programme of solidarity and equality as the basis for social integration. Throughout the history of industrial capitalism the first category towards which one might turn when faced with that question would be the labour movement, the combination of workers organized in trade unions and social democratic political parties. What is absolutely extraordinary in the last years of the twentieth century is that the labour movement is in such disarray. That disarray is of course something which is the product of political action directed exactly at creating it through making it virtually impossible for workers to win a strike.

This situation is particularly marked in the UK under Blair's leadership of 'New Labour'. Elsewhere there are more hopeful signs. The victory by the US Teamsters' Union under its reformist (i.e. anti-gangster) leadership, which forced the massive United Parcels Service to give permanent contracts and conditions to thousands of 'temporary' employees, was an outstanding example of a revived basic trade unionism which seems to be developing in that country. In France local coalitions among Greens, radical Catholics and post-Stalinist communists are the basis of a real opposition to globalizing tendencies. There are elements in the German and Swedish Social Democrats and in the left of the German Christian Democrats who are engaged in analysis and action on these issues. These forces are extremely important and it is clearly vital that they are drawn together in some way. The struggle against international globalizing post-industrialism has to be international.

The problem is the leadership of the parties of the left and centre but the crisis should shock even them, certainly the Jospins if not the Blairs, into a remembrance of things past. The Greens should come on board because their programme of social sustainability and a proper relationship with nature is absolutely dependent on a taming of the untrammelled logics of globalization and business.

Within the UK and Ireland the bodies with the clearest understanding of the real character of the issues are the Christian churches. It is necessary to impose a particular obligation on the churches for two reasons. The first is that given the clarity of their analysis, they are under a logical imperative to move towards some action on it. The second is that they represent not just a moral authority – in fact I am rather reluctant to cede any special moral authority to them – but also a considerable resource base. When we turn to issues of empowerment, a crucial problem will be that of seed funding, and in particular of seed funding which is independent of the state. The churches will have to put up initial cash and other organizational resources.

It is very important that the labour and Green movements and the churches are involved in any programme of action against exclusion, not only because of the resource and organizational base they offer but also because they provide means through which those who are excluded and who are at risk of exclusion can be brought together. This is why the status of the excluded as a reserve army of labour is so important. There is a real community of interest between the reserve army of labour and the mainstream because the purpose of the reserve army is to weaken the position of the mainstream. Of course the implication of the new international division of labour is that the reserve army is now global but that simply predicates a global internationalism rather than any fundamental disparity of interest in the long run. The great triumph of the labour movement in Britain and Ireland in the late nineteenth and early twentieth centuries was the creation of general unions which organized the disorganized. That remains a key linking objective for the future. Those in the USA who have disconnected the trade union movement from subordination to a Democratic Party which does not reflect its interests have an important lesson to deliver to the British labour movement. Let us turn now to issues of empowerment of the dispossessed themselves.

> The people here aren't the problem. They are the solution.
>
> (Holman in Borrie 1994: 306)

Holman's assertion forms the epigraph to a discussion of 'regeneration from the bottom up' which is Chapter 7 of the report of the Borrie Commission (1994). In the discussion of social exclusion in general and the excluding implications of urban development in particular, I have placed considerable emphasis on the role of process and have identified the decline of real democratic politics and the development of new corporatist forms as a crucial component of the disempowering and hence dispossession of the excluded. The word empowerment has been used to suggest an alternative approach. First, a note of caution. As Page (1992) reminds us, it is quite likely that some processes of empowerment do not mean much for the supposedly empowered:

> social work techniques of this kind may prove to be more beneficial to facilitators and educators who wish to cling on to the vestiges of a personally rewarding form of 'radical' practice rather than to those disadvantaged members of the community for whom the promise of a better tomorrow appears to be as far away as ever.
>
> (Page 1992: 92)

With that warning borne in mind, how might we develop a programme of real empowerment which might help those excluded and liable to exclusion in acting in a transformative way? The ideas of Freire (1973, 1977) are enormously useful here, particularly if read with the assistance of Heaney's (1995) very useful introduction and glossary. The significance of Freire's ideas about social pedagogy are immense because, in contrast to the Leninist account of the role of the party cadre who knows through the principles of 'scientific Marxism' what is right and has the task of raising the mere 'trade unionist' consciousness of the proletariat, for Freire pedagogy is always a process of mutual change and transformation. The idea is perhaps best expressed in Freire's conception of 'participatory research':

> Participatory research is an approach to social change – a process used by and for people who are exploited and oppressed. The approach challenges the way knowledge is produced with conventional social science methods and disseminated by dominant educational institutions. Through alternate methods, it puts the production of knowledge back into the hand of the people where it can infuse their struggles for social equality, and for the elimination of dependency and its symptoms: poverty, illiteracy, malnutrition etc.
>
> (Heaney 1995: 11)

The role of those with expertise in this can only be collegiate participation in empowerment: 'a consequence of liberatory learning. Power is not given, but created within the emerging praxis in which co-learners are engaged' (Heaney 1995: 10). The method must be dialogical: 'The dialogical approach to learning is characterised by co-operation and acceptance of interchangeability and mutuality in the roles of teacher and learner. In this method, all teach and all learn.' (Heaney 1995: 10).

There are very real problems for the development of action in the west which might be qualitatively different from those of Brazil, the real model for a politics which might confront globalism. Auyero's (1997) account of marginalization in Latin America is one of very considerable separation, of an almost uncrossable gulf. Whatever the disadvantages of that, and in Brazil its extent is clearly not such as to make it absolutely uncrossable, because otherwise the Workers' Party could not have unified the poor and the industrial working class, relatively permanent spatial exclusion generates a spatial stability of community. In advanced industrial societies, the spatial dynamics described in Chapter 6 mean that people can and do move on a programme of individual betterment.

Lemann (1991) has reviewed the experience of the Woodlawn Organization, often cited in the 1960s as the successful spatially based organization of the marginalized poor:

> the tide was running out in Woodlawn. Working-class people with reliable jobs – the one absolute necessity for a long-running community organization according to the Alinsky playbook – kept leaving for

better neighbourhoods to the south and west. Many of the Woodlawn Organization's members left as soon as they were able to . . .

The history of the Woodlawn Organization in Chicago was a perfect demonstration of the shortcomings of the empowerment theory in the real world of a late twentieth century American city: no matter how well organized a poor community was, it could not become stable and not poor so long as the people with good jobs kept moving out and the people left behind had very little income.

(Lemann 1991: 101, 122)

The poverty programmes of US President Lyndon B. Johnson's administration's Great Society initiative, a really genuine attempt to extend Fordist prosperity in a Fordist era, simply exacerbated the situation by creating a new cadre of public sector employees who 'used their new government paychecks to finance their relocation to better areas' (Lemann 1991: 251).

The National Government Minister Walter Runciman, whose family fortunes were founded on Tyneside shipping, made himself notorious in the 1930s by telling the people of Jarrow, 'the town that was murdered', that they must work out their own destiny. The poor of the excluded spaces of contemporary post-industrial capitalism cannot work out their destiny alone.

And nobody else can work it out without them! We are really facing a crisis here. It is perfectly obvious that untrammelled liberal capitalism doesn't work. It creates ecological disasters. It produces more than can be sold in a liberalized market. It renders the lives of the majority insecure and contingent while the superclass thrives.

So it is plainly time for an alliance of the many against the few. Given the nature of post-industrial politics and the capture of important parties of the left and centre by the superclass, this will not be easy. However, European Christian, Social Democratic, post-Leninist Communist and Green parties, the Brazilian Workers' Party, and member directed trade unions everywhere have a common cause with those who are dispossessed now.

There are three reasonable scenarios for the transformation of post-industrial capitalism into a social order with a prospect of medium term stability, of a period if not of economic growth then of social cohesion for perhaps the next thirty years. All must be redistributive since, to use the language of chaos/complexity, it is plain that a key controlling parameter for both the attractor states of whole social orders and for the ensembles of attractors of individual lives, for the intersections of history and biographies, is the degree of social inequality.

The first is a, necessarily global, revival of Keynesianism. In much of the world the deficits of social capital have not been rectified. Where they have, as in the societies of metropolitan capitalism, then there is an urgent need for collective expenditures on social care, not least because demography above all else has fractured the basis of intergenerational family care. Likewise there is a programme of ecological regeneration based on the proper employment of human labour. These activities will have to be funded from the revenues of tax collecting states. The taxes should come from the superclass.

Second, there is Hutton's (1995) Rhineland capitalism with its stakeholders. There is a problem with this. Essentially the corporatist arrangements of Rhineland capitalism are predicated on growth, not on redistribution. They are a method of getting the rising tide to lift all boats. It is perfectly possible to see the twenty-first century as an era of feasible growth, but only if the growth is measured in terms which are not derived solely from the accounts of capitalist production. Hutton and others have argued very strongly for the Rhineland route, but it is plainly vulnerable as an inherently capitalist led strategy, to the pressures of liberal globalizing capitalism. Investment in European stocks has boomed precisely because liberal market investors have seen a killing in stripping out all stakeholders but the shareholders from the Rhineland system.

Third, there is the old impossible dream of a popularly directed and planned production system – feasible socialism with a human face. Perhaps this has to have market elements as Nove (1983) cogently argued, but it is interesting to note that the very intellectual apparatus of chaos and complexity theory, associated with the technology of information processing, is making possible a collectivism which traditionally has seemed possible only under conditions of Asiatic despotism. Actually in the UK during the Second World War the economy was coordinated and organized on social lines without despotism, but the issue now is how to achieve a global justice, not simply a temporary condition in one nation facing a submarine blockade.

It is interesting that most discussion of a possible future politics against exclusion focuses on the national level. It is true that there is a European dialogue and that regional institutions in that very large part of Europe which now has a regional system in place, are concerned with the issue. We even have had some global level thinking and the proposal of international Keynesianism through the Brandt Commission's reports (1983, 1985). All these levels matter but I want to argue here for a specifically local level of action. It is true that there are some local initiatives. Some local authorities have anti-poverty strategies and there are local coalitions based on the voluntary sector which have at least held meetings to discuss the issue. However, in the UK, unlike France, there are not real political coalitions which demand that the fight for greater equality should dominate all policy formation and implementation.

In my view there is a great deal of mileage in using the idea of the 'sustainable city' as the basis for a local politics against exclusion. The Christian churches and the Greens must come together with local labour movement organizations, Trades Union Congress (TUC) (in the UK the funded 'Centres Against Unemployment') and community organizations to work out a real political strategy. This cannot be confined to attempting to influence policy makers. It must be prepared to put real pressure on them. The democratic process is in terrible trouble in post-industrial capitalism. A truly subsidiaristic local politics founded in civil society is absolutely necessary in order to revive it. My own view is that the regional level is also very important here. In the medium to long term, within one human generation, it is highly likely that the national level of states such as the UK and France will not matter very much. It is certainly desirable that this should happen. In a Europe of localities, regions and a European federal state, a real politics against exclusion should be possible. Note that I have no romantic notions about neighbourhoods as part of this system. Frankly, the very high levels of residential mobility out of areas of dispossession mean that any politics based on the neighbourhood level is far more likely to take the form of middle class NIMBYism (not in my back yard) than anything else. The local is a level which covers the span of post-industrial experiences. It is a basis for universalistic programmes, at least so far as the internal politics of metropolitan post-industrial capitalism are concerned.

So to conclude: social exclusion derives from inequality. It is a product of the post-industrial social order dominated by globalizing capital and the superclass associated with that globalizing capital. Attractive as the notion might be of watering the fields with the blood of the superclass, practically the way to deal with them is through two other forms of bloodletting – through the proper taxation of high incomes and accumulated wealth with the revenues used to sustain a process of global development on a sustainable basis, coupled with a restoration of basic organizational rights to workers so that they can both resist job instability and reduce the levels of corporate profits and senior executive remuneration to the benefit of wage earners. I think that the development of local coalitions against exclusion, popular fronts based on all social forces which are prepared to set solidarity as the key social goal, is a means towards the development of a political culture in which such a programme has some chance of being put into effect.

Notes

Introduction

1 Here the word 'determines' will always be used in the sense which is appropriate for a chaos/complexity understanding of the development of social systems. In summary 'determine' here means not to predict exactly, i.e. the linear conception of the term. Rather, at the level of the whole social system it means to create a complex form. For individuals, households, neighbourhoods, communities, localities and other higher order collectivities/spatial levels it means to allocate to broadly bounded but highly differentiated trajectories of condition and experience.

2 Note that a clear distinction is being made here between democratic socialism and 'democratic' centralism. That Leninist project in which the party, supposedly informed by its scientific grasp of an essentially mechanistic dialectical materialism, replaced the working class as collective agent, is now consigned to the dustbin of history. Democratic socialism is essentially founded in the autonomous activity of a self-organized working class.

3 'Real' in an explicitly realist metatheoretical sense as described by Sayer (1989).

4 We should note that the doctrine of predestination was rejected by a reform movement in late eighteenth-century Presbyterianism in Ulster and Scotland which underpinned some of the best and most progressive elements of the British Enlightenment, witness the theology, for example, of Robert Burns. This is the mainstream of modern Presbyterianism but not of the fundamentalist project of personal salvation exemplified by the doctrines of Ian Paisley's Free Presbyterians and their associated churches in the United States.

5 Note that under Pope John Paul II the Church admitted its error in the 1980s in its condemnation and execution (through the civil power) of Jan Huss. There has been no recantation of the condemnations of Luther and Calvin and quite right too. Those two deserve their anathemas.

6 The non-transformational accounts discussed in Chapter 2 do not deny the reality of exploitation. They are to be distinguished from Marxist accounts by their belief that a reformed capitalism, with at the most an acceptable level of exploitation, is a potentially available social order, an achievable attractor state to use the chaos/complexity vocabulary.

7 I was reminded of just how important Marxism was by the content of the brilliant BBC dramatization of the dying of Nye Bevan, founder of the UK National Health Service, *Food for Ravens*, which drew on his own speeches and writings as text. This was broadcast on BBC2 at 11.15 p.m. in the hope, I guess, that few would watch and be influenced by it.

8 The Mensheviks were the minority in the Russian Social Democratic Party in 1917 who argued for a gradual transformation of society against the Bolsheviks, abrupt revolutionary change.

9 The mainstream of Solidarity's contemporary programme is very close to that of the Bavarian Christian Social Union. It is conservative and often xenophobic but has a strong solidaristic element.

10 The dialogical approach to learning is characterized by co-operation and acceptance of interchangeability and mutuality in the roles of teacher and learner, demanding an atmosphere of mutual acceptance and trust. This contrasts with the anti-dialogical approach which emphasizes the teacher's side of the learning relationship and frequently results in one-way communiqués perpetuating domination and oppression. Without dialogue, there is no communication, and without communication, there can be no liberatory education.

(Heaney 1995: 12)

Chapter 1

1 The rejection of the programme of national reconstruction proposed by the Irish Commissioners and the introduction instead of an English style system had immediate effects in relation to the famine of the 1840s and long term effects in that Ireland, uniquely in the world, is a country with only half the population now that it had 150 years ago.

2 Dennis and Erdos (1992) is based on a re-examination of data from the Thousand Families study based on a cohort born in Newcastle in the 1940s. The weakness of their approach is illustrated by their own words: 'It has seldom been possible in our researches, even in very substantial and long term investigations, to assess the effects of social class and income independently of the commitment of a father' (Dennis and Erdos 1992: 36). Since they produce not one table in which the effects of class and income are controlled for, in assessing the impact of female headed single parenthood on children's lives, the correct statement would have been that 'it has never been possible in our researches'. In other words they encountered an empty cell problem: there were no affluent single mothers. This is not just a statistical artefact. It is a structural value – the technical expression for a necessary reflection of the nature of social reality in the period during which their sample grew up.

3 In *Farewell to the Working Class* Gorz (1982) argued that capital, through a series of managerialist strategies, technological innovations and spatial redeployments, has emancipated itself from labour, and that in consequence the working class is no longer a significant collective actor in the social order of late modernity.

Chapter 2

1 That Christian Democracy is anti-communist, and was originally anti-socialist, is obvious. However, it is not in principle about the restoration of the old conservative order. In post-Second World War Europe, traditional conservative forces

have generally regrouped within Christian Democratic parties, as have former fascists, but the project of Christian Democracy is one of modernity. The use of 'order' institutional forms, e.g. of Bismarckian insurance schemes, should not cause us to ignore the radical change involved in the assimilation of order liberalism to the Christian founded political project.

2 This is actually important in the UK as well. Figures as significant as John Wheatley, the first Labour Minister of Health, formed their life projects around exactly this reconciliation. However, the significance of political left Catholicism in the UK is generally ignored in academic study. It suffers under the double disadvantage of being too working class and too Irish.

3 The CCBI proposals are an interesting variant on the classic Keynesian techniques. Instead of emphasizing public sector capital formation through infrastructure development, the CCBI argues for a mix of environmental projects and labour intensive employment in health and social care. There is a lot to be said for this approach.

Chapter 3

1 The Speenhamland system was the best known of a variety of local schemes operating under the English Old Poor Law in which the low wages of agricultural labourers were supplemented in a formula depending on the size of their families and the price of bread.

2 This account is one founded in a 'complexity' approach after the development of those ideas by Reed and Harvey (1992, 1996). See Byrne (1998) for an exposition of them.

3 Jessop's (1994) work is of course meant to be description, but on reading 'New' Labour's proposals for the recasting of social policy one gets the impression that the people working in the policy units and Demos, 'New' Labour's tame think-tank, have read it as prescription.

4 This is dreadful anthropomorphism, but makes sense if we see 'capital' as the coalescence of the active interests of capitalists.

5 In Poland capitalist-style consumption and its representation has spread very rapidly since 1992 when I first visited the country. The real incomes of most Poles (even when all informal activities are taken into account) remain low by western European standards but they are still a significant market. Several of my Polish colleagues have become, either on a full- or part-time basis, those who market to them.

Chapter 4

1 New Labour, in a complete abandonment of one of the central tools of traditional Keynesian macro-economic politics, handed interest rate policy over to a central bank committee with a financial sector orientation. To quote the former Tory Chancellor Kenneth Clarke, a right Keynesian but definitely a Keynesian, the one club left in the golf bag has been given away.

2 Such data sets have been around for rather a long time. What is new are data sets which enable us to track the trajectory of households through time. Leisering and Walker (1998a) do recognize that cohort studies provide longitudinal accounts of individual life courses. What they miss is the significance of spatial longitudinal data sets, primarily census derived, which enable us to review the nature of socio-spatial trajectories for regions, localities and neighbourhoods.

3 Each set is a set of people. The set of sets is the overall categorization which we find by exploratory data analyses.
4 We often want to get within the household and look at the distribution of material resources inside it. This is particularly important for issues of gender and for the position of children. We return to this in Chapter 5.
5 Normally the idea of a butterfly attractor is used to describe the form of the trajectory of a single system which has two radically different very general states. Very small differences of initial condition can move the system from one of these general state to another. I am using the term here in a different way to describe the possible different trajectory domains of the components, individuals and households, who make up the atoms of a social system, and thereby see the attractor as describing the emergent form of the system as a whole, which is constituted by two separated domains within which the social atoms are located.

Chapter 5

1 Crompton makes a very similar point in her discussion of the advantages of log-linear techniques in studies of social mobility when she distinguishes this qualitative (in the sense of categorical/nominal levels of measurement) approach from the regression derived approach of path analysis which depends on continuous data because the former allows in '*structural* constraints which shape not only the occupational system but also processes of allocation within it' (Crompton 1993: 62, original emphasis).
2 This is a simplification because, as Ohlin-Wright (1985) reminds us, both Marx and Weber really employ production centred conceptions of class but 'The difference between them is that Weber views production from the vantage point of the market in which these assets are traded, whereas Marx views production from the vantage point of the exploitation it generates . . . this represents the fundamental difference between a culturalist and a materialist view of society' (Ohlin-Wright 1985: 107).
3 Possessive individualism is very important in relation to gender because it asserts the irrelevance of household arrangements for the taxation of individual incomes. Disaggregation of personal incomes has massively advantaged high income couples as households. At the other end of the scale there is an argument for disaggregation of course when we examine actual resource distributions within households where women (and now some men) are dependent spouses.
4 Far from demonstrating that long term inequality is not so severe as indicated by the changing character of income distribution taken alone, as is argued by Dennis (1997), this indicates the restoration of the good old Victorian value of insecurity and the Victorian condition of underemployment.
5 The argument for taking income after housing costs is based on the notion that the money payment for housing can increase without any real increase in living standards since there is no change in the substantive content of the accommodation. Dennis (1997) dismisses this, arguing that there has been a real increase in housing standards. There is more extensive provision of central heating in social housing but this in no way offsets the negative effective of the deterioration in the neighbourhood character of social housing. In any event the taking of income after housing costs reflects the fact that most poor people in the UK do not pay the costs of social housing because rents are either met directly or substantially discounted for those with low earnings.

6 US Census Bureau figures released in October 1997 showed that average US incomes were virtually the same as in 1973 (*Left Business Observer* February 1998). As Henwood (1998) puts it:

> almost all the benefits of economic growth, at least by official measures of inflation adjusted income, have gone to the richest 5 per cent of US households. The next 15 per cent have done well if not spectacularly, while the bottom 80 per cent have been lucky to stay in place . . . Because of this more people are working longer hours than at any time in modern history, which, while it helps keep up incomes, is hell on both home life and the public culture.
>
> (Henwood 1998: 3)

Absolute surplus value expropriation indeed!

7 Cantillon and Nolan (1998), who examined this issue in notoriously patriarchal Ireland, concluded that so far as financial resources as opposed to power about financial decision making was concerned, there is 'a limited overall imbalance of measured deprivation in favour of husbands' and that to 'apply such [standard household resource] indicators to individuals will not reveal a substantial reservoir of poverty among wives in non-poor households, nor much greater deprivation among women than men in poor households' (Cantillon and Nolan 1998: 151).

8 Efforts at enforcing the maintenance liabilities of fathers have not benefited the incomes of single mothers since in general any cash recovered from a benefit dependent single mother's former partner is offset against her benefit payments and she receives none of it. Working single mothers may benefit of course but they are much more likely to be in poorly paid part-time work and may well then lose part of any gain through taper mechanisms in means-tested supplements to low incomes.

9 Wright (1992, 1993) concludes that in the UK, while women are over-represented in the ranks of the poor, this gender based disadvantage has not increased over time. Hills (1995) confirmed a convergence of women's incomes towards men's coupled with a high degree of differentiation within each gender. Rubery and Fagan (1995) note the growing number of relatively mixed occupations in which gender segregation appears to be breaking down. For the USA, Orloff (1996) and Kodias and Jones (1991) argue that the representation of women and their dependent children among the poor is increasing. In Poland Grolowska-Leder and Warzyswoda-Kruszynska (1997) show that unemployment contingent on restructuring is differentially impacting on women, and this, coupled with the familiast attitudes of the Catholic Church and reduction in state provision of child care, is increasing both the absolute and relative incidence of female poverty.

10 The notion of ethnicity being employed in this chapter is Barth's (1969). It emphasizes social identification and argues that the discontinuities among ethnic groups are to be understood in social rather than cultural terms.

11 This term is the least contentious as a distinguishing expression since it describes the set of those who did not record themselves as 'white' in the UK 1991 Census but used one of the other categories which combined ethnicity and national origin. There are political reasons for using the term 'black' generically but many people of South Asian origin reject it.

12 There is a lot of racism in the UK – witness the racist murder of Stephen Lawrence, a black teenager killed in a London street. However, racist exclusion is not a central principle of social life.

13 Ironically, Dr DeAnne Julius despite her publicly expressed view that advanced economies should progress towards a service base, was the only member of the

committee to vote for reduced interest rates in order to maintain the manufacturing base in August 1998.

14 McCrate and Smith (1998) remark of the 1996 US 'Personal Responsibility and Work Opportunity Reconciliation Act' that: 'The structural changes are profound: they effectively destroy one of the major pillars of the New Deal' (1998: 61). McCrate and Smith also note that when similar measures were introduced at a state level in Vermont, the majority of those involved in the promotion of such measures were affluent women administrators and legislators.

Chapter 6

1 There is an equally significant spatial concentration and segregation of the affluent, but given social science's general posture of hands turned up for the money and eyes down for the surveilling gaze, we do not usually pay much attention to that, not since Thorstein Veblen (1972 [1908]) anyway.

2 I mean one conducted using multivariate classificatory procedures which allow us to explore the character of variation in urban space. In other words I do not mean approaches using factor analysis or its derivatives which are founded around a notion of hidden causal elements.

3 By 'councillor' I mean an elected representative – not a therapist.

4 To quote one 70-year-old woman who was one of my constituents: 'I don't mind them having a sex life. I was in the Wrens for five years and I think there would be something wrong with them if they didn't. All I ask is they keep it quiet!' Divorcees in their late twenties and thirties were very popular neighbours – steady, reliable and discreet.

5 Housing managers knew where people came from since they were obliged to give their last address on their application forms. They did try to find where people went to but there was no similar record and no obligation on a tenant in good standing to give this information to housing managers.

Conclusion

1 'See, Judge, Act' was and is the programme of the Young Christian Workers of which I was a member in the early 1960s. It still seems a good programme to me.

2 Stubbs (1991) shows that builders in Sunderland (North East England) in the late 1950s and early 1960s targeted their advertising for new speculative housing on the more prosperous council tenants pointing out that buying was only marginally more expensive than renting and involved the accumulation of a capital asset. Then most council tenant households in Sunderland depended solely on wages. Now more than 60 per cent of households with children in council tenure in that city have incomes so low that all or part of their rent is remitted.

Bibliography

Allen, J. (1998) Europe of the neighbourhoods: class, citizenship and welfare regimes, in A. Madanipour, G. Cars and J. Allen (eds) *Social Exclusion in European Cities*. London: Jessica Kingsley.

Amin, A. (ed.) (1994) *Post-Fordism: A Reader*. Oxford: Blackwell.

Anderson, J., Duncan, S. and Hudson, R. (1983) *Redundant Spaces in Cities and Regions*. London: Academic Press.

Arendt, H. (1958) *The Origins of Totalitarianism*. London: Allen & Unwin.

Ashworth, K., Hill, M. and Walker, R. (1994) Patterns of childhood poverty, *Journal of Policy Analysis and Management*, 13 (4): 658–80.

Atkinson, A.B. (1995) *Incomes and the Welfare State*. Cambridge: Cambridge University Press.

Atkinson, A.B., Rainwater, L. and Smeeding, T.M. (1995) *Income Distribution in OECD Countries*. Paris: Organization for Economic Cooperation and Development.

Audit Commission (1996) *Misspent Youth*. London: HMSO.

Auyero, J. (1997) Wacquant in the Argentine Slums, *International Journal of Urban and Regional Research*, 27 (2): 508–11.

Ball, S.J., Bowe, R. and Gewirtz, S. (1995) Circuits of schooling, *Sociological Review*, 43: 52–78.

Banim, M. (1986) Occupying houses: the social relations of tenure. Unpublished PhD thesis, University of Durham.

Bankston, C. and Caldas, S.J. (1996) Majority African American schools and social injustice: the influence of de facto segregation on academic achievement, *Social Forces*, 75 (2): 535–55.

Barth, F. (ed.) (1969) *Ethnic Groups and Boundaries: The Social Organization of Culture Difference*. Oslo: Universitetsforlaget.

Bartley, B. (1998) Exclusion, invisibility and the neighbourhood in West Dublin, in A. Madanipour, G. Cars and J. Allen (eds) *Social Exclusion in European Cities*. London: Jessica Kingsley.

Bauman, Z. (1987) From here to modernity, *New Statesman*, 25 September.

Bauman, Z. (1997) No way back to bliss: how to cope with the restless chaos of modernity, *Times Literary Supplement*, 24 January.

Bauman, Z. (1998) *Work, Consumerism and the New Poor.* Buckingham: Open University Press.

Berlin, I. (1969) *Four Essays on Liberty.* London: Oxford University Press.

Bessis, S. (1995) From social exclusion to social cohesion: a policy agenda. MOST Policy Paper no. 2 http://www.unesco.org/most/besseng.htm

Beveridge, W.H. (1944) *Full Employment in a Free Society.* London: Allen & Unwin.

Blair, T. (1998) *The Third Way: New Politics for the New Century.* London: Fabian Society.

Bluestone, B. and Harrison, B. (1982) *The Deindustrialization of America.* New York: Basic Books.

Borrie, G. (chair) (1994) *Social Justice.* London: Vintage.

Bourdieu, P. (1990) *The Logic of Practice.* Cambridge: Polity.

Brandt Commission (1983) *Common Crisis.* London: Pan.

Brandt Commission (1985) *Global Challenge.* London: Pan.

Braun, D. (1997) *The Rich Get Richer.* Chicago: Nelson-Hall.

Braverman, H. (1974) *Labor and Monopoly Capital,* foreword by Paul M. Sweezy. New York: Monthly Review Press.

Brown, P. (1995) Cultural capital and social exclusion, *Work, Employment and Society,* 9: 29–52.

Byrne, D.S. (1984) Dublin – a case study of housing and the residual working class, *International Journal of Urban and Regional Research,* 3: 402–20.

Byrne, D.S. (1989a) *Beyond the Inner City.* Milton Keynes: Open University Press.

Byrne, D.S. (1989b) Sociotenurial polarization: issues of production and consumption in a locality, *International Journal of Urban and Regional Research,* 13 (3): 369–89.

Byrne, D.S. (1995) Deindustrialization and dispossession, *Sociology,* 29: 95–116.

Byrne, D.S. (1997a) Chaotic places or complex places: cities in a post-industrial era, in S. Westwood and J. Williams (eds) *Imagining Cities: Scripts, Signs, Memory.* London: Routledge.

Byrne, D.S. (1997b) Social exclusion and capitalism, *Critical Social Policy,* 17 (1): 27–51.

Byrne, D.S. (1998) *Complexity Theory and the Social Sciences.* London: Routledge.

Byrne, D.S. (1999) Tyne and Wear UDC: turning the uses inside out – active deindustrialisation and its consequences, in R. Imrie and H. Thomas (eds) *British Urban Policy and the Urban Development Corporation,* 2nd edn. London: Paul Chapman.

Byrne, D.S. and Parson, D. (1983) The state and the reserve army, in J. Anderson, S. Duncan and R. Hudson (eds) *Redundant Spaces in Cities and Regions.* London: Academic Press.

Byrne, D.S. and Rogers, T. (1996) Divided spaces: divided school, *Sociological Research Online* 1 http://Kennedy.soc.surrey.ac.uk/socresonline/1/2/contents.html

Byrne, D.S. and Wodz, K. (1997) La désindustrialization dans les villes industrielles en déclin, in A. Martens and M. Vervaeke (eds) *La polarisation sociale des villes européenes.* Paris: Anthropos.

Cabinet Office Social Exclusion Unit (1998) *Bringing Britain Together: a National Strategy for Neighbourhood Renewal.* London: HMSO.

Callaghan, G. (1998) Deindustrialization, class and gender: young adults in Sunderland. Unpublished PhD thesis, University of Durham.

Cantillon, S. and Nolan, B. (1998) Are married women more deprived than their husbands? *Journal of Social Policy,* 27 (2): 151–71.

Catholic Bishops' Conference of England and Wales (1996) *The Common Good.* London: Catholic Bishops' Conference.

Chance, J. (1997) The Irish: invisible settlers, in C. Peach (ed.) *The Ethnic Minority Populations of Great Britain, Ethnicity in the 1997 Census,* vol. 2. London: HMSO.

Cleaver, H. (1977) Malaria, the politics of public health and the international crisis, *Review of Radical Political Economy*, 9: 81–103.

Cleaver, H. (1979) *Reading Capital Politically*. Brighton: Harvester Wheatsheaf.

Coleman, D. and Salt, J. (eds) (1996) *Ethnicity in the 1991 Census: Volume One: Demographic Characteristics*. London: HMSO.

Council of Churches for Great Britain and Ireland (CCBI) (1997) *Unemployment and the Future of Work*. London: CCBI.

Crompton, R. (1993) *Class and Stratification*. Cambridge: Polity.

Crouch, C. and Marquand, D. (1989) *The New Centralism: Britain Out of Step in Europe*. Oxford: Blackwell.

Crowe, G. and Allan, G. (1994) *Community Life*. Hemel Hempstead: Harvester Wheatsheaf.

Dahrendorf, R. (1987) The erosion of citizenship and its consequences for us all, *New Statesman*, 12 June: 12–15.

Dahrendorf, R. (chair) (1995) *Report on Wealth Creation and Social Cohesion in a Free Society*. London: Commission on Wealth Creation and Social Cohesion.

Damer, S. (1989) *From Moorepark to 'Wine Alley': The Rise and Fall of a Glasgow Housing Scheme*. Edinburgh: Edinburgh University Press.

Danson, M. and Mooncy, G. (1998) Glasgow: a tale of two cities?, in P. Lawless, R. Martin and S. Hardy (eds) *Unemployment and Social Exclusion*. London: Jessica Kingsley.

Davies, J.G. (1974) *The Evangelistic Bureaucrats*. London: Tavistock.

Deacon, B. (1997) *Global Social Policy*. London: Sage.

Dennis, N. (1997) *The Invention of Permanent Poverty*. London: Institute of Economic Affairs.

Dennis, N. and Erdos, G. (1992) *Families without Fatherhood*. London: Institute of Economic Affairs.

Domanskia, H. (1994) Nowe mechanizmy stratyfikacyjne? *Studia Socjologicsne*, 132 (1): 53–76.

Donnison, D. (1998) *Policies for a Just Society*. London: Macmillan.

Douglas, J.W.B. (1968) *All our Future*. London: Peter Davies.

Driver, S. and Martell, L. (1997) New Labour's communitarianisms, *Critical Social Policy*, 17 (3): 27–46.

Duffy, K. (1997) *Review of the International Dimensions of the Thematic Priority on Social Integration and Exclusion: A Report to the UK Economic and Social Research Council*. Leicester: De Montfort University.

Duncan, G.J., Smeeding, T.M. and Rodgers, W. (1992) The incredible shrinking middle class, *American Demographics*, 14 May: 34–8.

Duncan, G.J., Smeeding, T.M. and Rodgers, W. (1993) W(h)ither the middle class? A dynamic view, in D.B. Papadimitriou and E.N. Wolff (eds) *Poverty and Prosperity in the USA in the Late Twentieth Century*. London: Macmillan.

Economic and Social Research Council (ESRC) (1996) *Thematic Priorities*. Swindon: ESRC.

Eder, K. (1993) *The New Politics of Class*. London: Sage.

Ellison, N. (1997) Towards a new social politics: citizenship and reflexivity in late modernity, *Sociology*, 31 (4): 697–717.

Engels, F. (1968) *The Condition of the Working Classes in England in 1844*. London: Allen & Unwin.

Erikson, R. and Goldthorpe, J.H. (1992) *The Constant Flux*. Oxford: Clarendon Press.

Esping-Andersen, G. (1990) *The Three Worlds of Welfare Capitalism*. Cambridge: Polity.

Esser, J. and Hirsch, J. (1994) The crisis of Fordism and the dimensions of a 'post-Fordist' regional and urban structure, in A. Amin (ed.) *Post-Fordism*. Oxford: Blackwell.

Etzioni, A. (1995) *The Spirit of Community*. London: Fontana.

European Commission (1994) *Growth, Competitiveness and Employment*. Luxemburg: Office for Official Publications of the European Communities.

European Commission DGV (1994) *European Social Policy: A Way Forward for the Union*. Luxemburg: Office for Official Publications of the European Communities.

Eversley, D. (1990) Inequality at the spatial level: tasks for planners, *The Planner*, 76 (30 March): 12.

Fainstein, S. and Harloe, M. (1992) Introduction: London and New York in the contemporary world, in S. Fainstein, I. Gordon and M. Harloe (eds) *Divided Cities*. Oxford: Blackwell.

Fainstein, S., Gordon, I. and Harloe, M. (eds) (1992) *Divided Cities: New York and London in the Contemporary World*. Oxford: Blackwell.

Field, F. (1996) *Stakeholder Welfare*. London: Institute of Economic Affairs.

Fitch, R. (1993) *The Assassination of New York*. London: Verso.

Ford, R. and Miller, J. (eds) (1998a) *Private Lives and Public Responses*. London: Policy Studies Institute.

Ford, R. and Miller, J. (1998b) Lone parenthood in the UK: policy dilemmas and solutions, in R. Ford and J. Miller (eds) *Private Lives and Public Responses*. London: Policy Studies Institute.

Freire, P. (1973) *Education: The Practice of Freedom*. London: Writers' and Readers' Publishing Cooperative.

Freire, P. (1977) *Cultural Action for Freedom*. Harmondsworth: Penguin.

Freire, P. (1982) *The Pedagogy of the Oppressed*. Harmondsworth: Penguin.

Friedman, M. (1982) *Capitalism and Freedom*. Chicago: University of Chicago Press.

Friend, A. and Metcalf, A. (1981) *Slump City: The Politics of Mass Unemployment*. London: Pluto Press.

Geddes, M. (1997) *Partnership against Poverty and Exclusion?* Bristol: Policy Press.

Goodman, A., Johnson, P. and Webb, S. (1997) *Inequality in the UK*. Oxford: Oxford University Press.

Gorz, A. (1982) *Farewell to the Working Class*. London: Pluto Press.

Gorzelak, G. (1996) *The Regional Dimension of Transformation in Poland*. London: Jessica Kingsley.

Gosling, A., Johnson, P., McCrae, J. and Paull, G. (1997) *The Dynamics of Low Pay and Unemployment in Early 1990s Britain*. London: Institute for Fiscal Studies.

Gowan, P. and Anderson, P. (eds) (1997) *The Question of Europe*. London: Verso.

Graham, J. (1992) Post-Fordism as politics: the political consequences of narratives on the left, *Environment and Planning D – Society and Space*, 10 (4): 393–410.

Green, A. (1997) *Housing, Family and Working Lives*. Coventry: Institute of Employment Research, University of Warwick.

Green, D. (1996) *Community without Politics*. London: Institute of Economic Affairs.

Green, D. (1998) *Benefit Dependency*. London: Institute of Economic Affairs.

Grolowska-Leder, J. and Warzywoda-Kruszynska, W. (1997) Women in the welfare state of Poland. Conference paper, European Sociological Association, Colchester, 5 September.

Guattari, F. and Negri, T. (1990) *Communists Like Us: New Spaces of Liberty, New Lines of Alliance*. New York: Semiotext(e).

Gulbenkian Commission (1996) *Open the Social Sciences: Report of the Gulbenkian Commission on the Restructuring of the Social Sciences*. Stanford: Stanford University Press.

Hamnett, C. (1994) Social polarization in global cities, *Urban Studies*, 31 (3): 401–24.

Hamnett, C. (1996) Social polarization, economic restructuring, and welfare state regimes, *Urban Studies*, 33 (8): 1407–30.

Hamnett, C. (1997) A stroke of the Chancellor's pen: the social and regional impact of the Conservative's 1988 higher tax rate cuts, *Environment and Planning A*, 29 (1) 129–47.

Harris, N. (1987) *The End of the Third World*. Harmondsworth: Penguin

Harrison, P. (1982) *Inside the Inner City*. Harmondsworth: Penguin.

Harvey, D.L. (1993) *Potter Addition*. New York: Aldine de Gruyter.

Harvey, D.L. and Reed, M.H. (1996) The culture of poverty: an ideological analysis, *Sociological Perspectives*, 39 (4): 465–95.

Hayek, F. (1944) *The Road to Serfdom*. London: Routledge and Kegan Paul.

Hazlitt, W. (1982) *Selected Writings*. Harmondsworth: Penguin.

Heady, C. (1997) Labour market transitions and social exclusion, *Journal of European Social Policy*, 7 (2): 119–28.

Heald, D. (1983) *Public Expenditure*. Oxford: Martin Robertson.

Heaney, T. (1995) *Issues in Freirean Pedagogy*. http://nlu.nl.edu/ace/Resources/FreireIssues.html

Heeny, E. (1997) Annual review article, *British Journal of Industrial Relations*, 35 (1): 87–109.

Heilbroner, R. (1993) *Twenty First Century Capitalism*. London: UCL Press.

Heisler, B.S. (1991) A comparative perspective on the underclass, *Theory and Society*, 20 (4): 455–83.

Henwood, D. (1998) Income and poverty. *Left Business Observer*. http://www.panix.com/~dhenwood/Stats_incpov.html

Herrnstein, R.J. and Murray, C. (1994) *The Bell Curve: Intelligence and Class Structure in American Life*. New York: Free Press.

Hill, M., Hill, D. and Walker, R. (1998) Intergenerational dynamics in the USA: poverty processes in young adulthood, in L. Leisering and R. Walker (eds) *The Dynamics of Modern Society*. Bristol: Policy Press.

Hills, J. (1995) *Joseph Rowntree Foundation Inquiry into Income and Wealth*, vol. 2. York: Joseph Rowntree Foundation.

Hills, J. (ed.) (1996) *The New Inequalities*. Cambridge: Cambridge University Press.

HM Treasury (1997) *The Modernisation of Britain's Tax and Benefit System: Employment Opportunity in a Changing Labour Market*. http://www.hm-treasury.gov.uk/pub/html/docs/fpp/mtb/main.html

Hudson, W.H. (1981 [1910]) *A Shepherd's Life*. London: Futura.

Hughes, M.A. (1989) Mis-speaking truth to power: a geographical perspective on the underclass fallacy, *Economic Geography*, 65: 189–207.

Hunt, E.K. and Schwartz, J.G. (eds) (1972) *A Critique of Economic Theory*. Harmondsworth: Penguin.

Hutton, W. (1995) *The State We're In*. London: Jonathan Cape.

Hutton, W. (1997a) *The State to Come*. London: Vintage.

Hutton, W. (1997b) *Stakeholding and its Critics*. London: Institute of Economic Affairs.

Imrie, R. and Thomas, H. (eds) (1999) *British Urban Policy and the Urban Development Corporations*, 2nd edn. London: Paul Chapman.

Inglis, B. (1972) *Poverty and the Industrial Revolution*. London: Panther.

Inglot, T. (1995) The politics of social policy reform in postcommunist Poland, *Communist and Postcommunist Studies*, 28 (3): 361–73.

James, C.L.R. (1986 [1950]) *State Capitalism and World Revolution*. Chicago: Charles H. Kerr.

Jenkins, S. (1995) Accounting for inequality trends. *Economica* 62: 29–63.

Jessop, B. (1994) Post-Fordism and the state, in A. Amin (ed.) *Post-Fordism*. Oxford: Blackwell.

Johnson, P. and Webb, S. (1993) Explaining the growth in UK income inequality, *Economic Journal*, 103: 429–35.

Jordan, B. (1996) *A Theory of Poverty and Social Exclusion.* Cambridge: Polity.

Karn, V. (ed.) (1997) *Employment, Education and Housing Among the Ethnic Minority Populations of Britain, Ethnicity in the 1991 Census,* vol. 4. London: Stationery Office.

Kempson, E. (1996) *Life on a Low Income.* York: Joseph Rowntree Foundation.

Kiel, L.D. and Elliott, E. (eds) (1996) *Chaos Theory in the Social Sciences.* Ann Arbor, MI: University of Michigan Press.

King, A. (1996) Introduction: cities, texts and paradigms, in A. King (ed.) *Re-Presenting the City.* London: Routledge.

Kodias, J.E. and Jones III, J.P. (1991) A contextual examination of the feminization of poverty, *Geoforum,* 22 (2): 159–71.

Küng, H. (1997) *A Global Ethic for Global Politics and Economics.* London: SCM Press.

Lash, S. and Urry, J. (1994) *Economies of Signs and Space.* London: Sage.

Lavery, G., Pender, J. and Peters, M. (eds) (1997) *Exclusion and Inclusion: Minorities in Europe.* Leeds: ISPRU Publications, Leeds Metropolitan University.

Lawless, P., Martin, R. and Hardy, S. (eds) (1998) *Unemployment and Social Exclusion.* London: Jessica Kingsley.

Lee, R. (1995) Look after the pounds and the people will look after themselves, *Environment and Planning A,* 27: 1577–94.

Leisering, L. and Walker, R. (eds) (1998a) *The Dynamics of Modern Society.* Bristol: Policy Press.

Leisering, L. and Walker, R. (1998b) New realities: the dynamics of modernity, in L. Leisering and R. Walker (eds) *The Dynamics of Modern Society.* Bristol: Policy Press.

Lemann, N. (1991) *The Promised Land.* London: Macmillan.

Levitas, R. (1996) The concept of social exclusion and the new Durkheimian hegemony, *Critical Social Policy,* 16 (1): 5–20.

Lewis, G. (1836) *Report on the State of the Irish Poor in Great Britain.* London: HMSO.

Lewis, O. (1966) *La Vida.* New York: Random House.

Lipietz, A. (1994) Post-Fordism and democracy, in A. Amin (ed.) *Post-Fordism.* Oxford: Blackwell.

Lipietz, A. (1998) Rethinking social housing in the hour-glass society, in A. Madanipour, G. Cars and J. Allen (eds) *Social Exclusion in European Cities.* London: Jessica Kingsley.

Lister, R. (1998) *Citizenship: Feminist Perspectives.* London: Macmillan.

Luttwak, E. (1997) Central Bankism, in P. Gowan and P. Anderson (eds) *The Question of Europe.* London: Verso.

McCrate, E. and Smith, J. (1998) When work doesn't work, *Gender and Society,* 12 (1): 61–80.

MacDonald, R. (ed.) (1997) *Youth, the 'Underclass' and Social Exclusion.* London: Routledge.

MacKay, R.R. (1998) Unemployment as exclusion: unemployment as choice, in P. Lawless, R. Martin and S. Hardy (eds) *Unemployment and Social Exclusion.* London: Jessica Kingsley.

McKay, S. (1998) Exploring the dynamics of family change: lone parenthood in Britain, in L. Leisering and R. Walker (eds) *The Dynamics of Modern Society.* Bristol: Policy Press.

MacNicol, J. (1987) In pursuit of the underclass, *Journal of Social Policy,* 16 (3): 293–318.

MacPherson, C.B. (1962) *The Political Theory of Possessive Individualism.* Oxford: Clarendon Press.

Madanipour, A. (1998) Social exclusion and space, in A. Madanipour, G. Cars and J. Allen (eds) *Social Exclusion in European Cities.* London: Jessica Kingsley.

Madanipour, A., Cars, G. and Allen, J. (eds) (1998) *Social Exclusion in European Cities*. London: Jessica Kingsley.

Marcuse, P. (1989) Dual city: a muddled metaphor for the quartered city, *International Journal of Urban and Regional Research*, 13 (4): 697–708.

Marris, R. (1996) *How to Save the Underclass*. London: Macmillan.

Marshall, T.H. (1950) *Citizenship and Social Class*. Cambridge: Cambridge University Press.

Martin, C. (1996) The debate in France over social exclusion, *Social Policy and Administration*, 30 (4): 382–92.

Martin, R. and Rowthorn, B. (eds) (1986) *The Geography of De-industrialisation*. London: Macmillan.

Marx, K. (1977 [1867]) *Das Kapital Volume 1*. Moscow: Progress Publishers.

Massey, D. and Denton, N.A. (1993) *American Apartheid*. London: Harvard University Press.

Maxwell, A.H. (1993) The underclass, 'social isolation' and 'concentration effects', *Current Anthropology*, 13 (3): 231–45.

Mead, L. (1988) *Beyond Entitlement: the Social Obligations of Citizenship*. New York: Free Press.

Mead, L.M. (1997) *From Welfare to Work*. London: Institute of Economic Affairs.

Meadows, P. (ed.) (1996) *Work Out – or Work In?* York: Joseph Rowntree Foundation.

Meiksins Wood, E. (1986) *The Retreat from Class*. London: Verso.

Merrett, S. (1979) *State Housing in Britain*. London: Routledge and Kegan Paul.

Millard, F. (1997) The influence of the Catholic hierarchy in Poland 1989–96, *Journal of European Social Policy*, 7 (2): 83–100.

Mills, C.W. (1959) *The Sociological Imagination*. New York: Oxford University Press.

Mingione, E. (ed.) (1996) *Urban Poverty and the Underclass*. Oxford: Blackwell.

Morenoff, J.D. and Tienda, M. (1997) Underclass neighbourhoods in temporal and ecological perspective, *Annals of the American Academy of Political and Social Science*, 551: 59–72.

Morris, L. and Scott, J. (1996) The attenuation of class analysis: comments, *British Journal of Sociology*, 47 (1): 45–55.

Moynihan, D.P. (1965) *The Negro Family: The Case for National Action*. Washington, DC: Department of Labor.

Murray, C. (1984) *Losing Ground*. New York: Basic Books.

Murray, C. (1990) *The Emerging British Underclass*. London: Institute of Economic Affairs.

Murray, C. (1994) *The Underclass: The Crisis Deepens*. London: Institute of Economic Affairs.

Negri, T. (1988) *Revolution Retrieved*. London: Red Notes.

Nelson, J.I. (1995) *Post-Industrial Capitalism*. London: Sage.

Nove, A. (1983) *The Economics of Feasible Socialism*. London: Allen & Unwin.

Nozick, R. (1974) *Anarchy, State and Utopia*. Oxford: Blackwell.

O'Connor, J. (1981) The meaning of crisis, *International Journal of Urban and Regional Research*, 5 (3): 301–29.

Ohlin-Wright, E. (1985) *Classes*. London: Verso.

Orloff, A. (1996) Gender in the welfare state, *Annual Review of Sociology*, 22: 51–78.

Page, R. (1992) Empowerment, oppression and beyond: a coherent strategy? *Critical Social Policy*, 35: 89–92.

Pahl, R. (1984) *Divisions of Labour*. Oxford: Blackwell.

Papadimitriou, D. (ed.) (1994) *Aspects of Distribution of Wealth and Income*. London: Macmillan.

Papadimitriou, D. and Wolff, E.N. (1993) *Poverty and Prosperity in the USA in the Late Twentieth Century*. London: Macmillan.

Parker, H. (1989) *Instead of the Dole*. London: Routeldge.

Paulin, T. (1998) *The Day-star of Liberty: William Hazlitt's Radical Style*. London: Faber.

Peach, C. (ed.) (1996) *The Ethnic Minority Populations of Great Britain, Ethnicity in the 1991 Census*, vol. 2. London: HMSO.

Peck, J. and Tickell, A. (1994) Searching for a new institutional fix: the *after*-Fordist crisis and global–local disorder, in A. Amin (ed.) *Post-Fordism*. Oxford: Blackwell.

Peterson, P.E. (1992) The urban underclass and the poverty paradox, *Political Science Quarterly*, 106: 617–37.

Pinch, S. (1993) Social polarization: a comparison of evidence from Britain and the United States, *Environment and Planning A*, 25: 779–95.

Prigogine, I. and Stengers, I. (1985) *Order Out of Chaos*. London: Flamingo.

Pryke, R. (1995) *Taking the Measure of Poverty*. London: Institute of Economic Affairs.

Reed, M. and Harvey, D.L. (1992) The new science and the old: complexity and realism in the social sciences, *Journal for the Theory of Social Research*, 22: 353–80.

Reed, M. and Harvey, D.L. (1996) Social science as the study of complex systems, in L.D. Kiel and E. Elliott (eds) *Chaos Theory in the Social Sciences*. Ann Arbor, MI: University of Michigan Press.

Rex, J. (1973) *Race, Colonialism and the City*. London: Routledge and Kegan Paul.

Ridley, N. (1987) *Department of the Enviroment Observations by the Government on the Third Report of the Employment Committee*, HC 83: 88–9. London: HMSO.

Robinson, F., Lawrence, M. and Shaw, K. (1994) *More than Bricks and Mortar*. York: Joseph Rowntree Trust.

Roche, M. (1992) *Rethinking Citizenship*. Cambridge: Polity.

Rodgers, J.R. (1994) The relationship between poverty and household type, in D. Papadimitriou (ed.) *Aspects of Distribution of Wealth and Income*. London: Macmillan.

Room, G. (ed.) (1995) *Beyond the Threshold*. Bristol: Policy Press.

Rose, H.M. (1991) The underclass debate goes on, *Urban Geography*, 12: 491–3.

Rose, N. (1996) The death of the social: refiguring the territory of government, *Economy and Society*, 25 (3): 327–56.

Rowlingson, K. and McKay, S. (1998) *The Growth of Lone Parenthood*. London: Policy Studies Institute.

Rubery, J. and Fagan, C. (1995) Gender segregation in societal context, *Work, Employment and Society*, 9 (2): 213–40.

Saunders, P. (1984) Beyond housing classes, *International Journal of Urban and Regional Research*, 8: 202–7.

Saunders, P. (1986) Comment on Pretceille and Dunleavy, *Society and Space*, 4: 155–63.

Saunders, P. (1996) *Unequal but Fair*. London: IEA.

Sayer, A. (1989) *Method in Social Science*. London: Routledge.

Sayer, A. (1995) Liberalism, Marxism and urban and regional studies, *International Journal of Urban and Regional Research*, 19 (1): 79–95.

Serge, V. (1978) *Captive City*. London: Writers' and Readers' Co-operative.

Silver, H. (1993) National conceptions and the new urban poverty, *International Journal of Urban and Regional Research*, 17 (3): 336–54.

Silver, H. (1994) Social exclusion and social solidarity: three paradigms, *International Labour Review*, 133: 531–78.

Smith, S. (ed.) (1991) *Economic Policy and the Division of Income within the Family*. London: Institute for Fiscal Studies.

Starrels, M.E., Bould, S. and Nicholas, L.J. (1994) The feminization of poverty in the United States, *Journal of Family Issues*, 15 (4): 590–607.

Stubbs, C. (1991) The state of tenure. Unpublished PhD thesis, University of Durham.

Teague, P. and Wilson, D. (1995) *Social Exclusion: Social Inclusion*. Belfast: Democratic Dialogue.

Therborn, G. (1985) *Why Some Peoples are More Unemployed than Others*. London: Verso.

Therborn, G. (1995) *European Modernity and Beyond*. London: Sage.

Thomas, S.L. (1994) From the culture of poverty to the culture of single motherhood, *Women and Politics*, 14 (2): 65–97.

Thompson, E.P. (1963) *The Making of the English Working Class*. London: Gollancz.

Thompson, E.P. (1975) *Whigs and Hunters*. London: Allen Lane.

Thompson, S. and Hoggett, P. (1996) Universalism, selectivism and particularism, *Critical Social Policy*, 16 (1): 21–43.

Titmuss, R.M. (1958) The social division of welfare, in R.M. Titmuss, *Essays of 'The Welfare State'*. London: Allen & Unwin.

Townsend, P. (1979) *Poverty in the United Kingdom*. Harmondsworth: Penguin.

Turner, B.S. (ed.) (1993) *Citizenship and Social Theory*. London: Sage.

United Nations Development Programme (UNDP) (1996) *Katowice Human Development Report 1996*. Katowice: UNDP.

Valentine, C. (1967) *Culture and Poverty*. Chicago: University of Chicago Press.

Veblen, T. (1972 [1908]) Professor Clark's Economics, *Quarterly Journal of Economics*, 22: 147–95: reprinted in E.K. Hunt and J.G. Schwartz (eds) *A Critique of Economic Theory*. Harmondsworth: Penguin.

Veit-Wilson, J. (1998) *Setting Adequacy Standards*. Bristol: Policy Press.

Wacquant, L.D. (1993) Urban outcasts: stigma and division in the Black American ghetto and the French urban periphery, *International Journal of Urban and Regional Research*, 17 (3): 366–83.

Wacquant, L.D. (1996) Red Belt, Black Belt: racial division, class inequality and the state in the French urban periphery and the American ghetto, in E. Mingione (ed.) *Urban Poverty and the Underclass*. Oxford: Blackwell.

Wacquant, L. and Wilson, W.J. (1989) The cost of racial and class exclusion in the inner city, *Annals of the American Academy of Political and Social Science*, 501: 8–25.

Walker, A. and Walker, C. (eds) (1997) *Britain Divided: The Growth of Social Exclusion in the 1980s and 1990s*. London: Child Poverty Action Group.

Walker, R. (1995) The dynamics of poverty and social exclusion, in G. Room (ed.) *Beyond the Threshold*. Bristol: Policy Press.

Walker, R. (1997) Poverty and social exclusion in Europe, in A. Walker and C. Walker (eds) *Britain Divided*. London: Child Poverty Action Group.

Walker, R. and Leisering, L. (1998) New tools: towards a dynamic science of modern society, in L. Leisering and R. Walker (eds) *The Dynamics of Modern Society*. Bristol: Policy Press.

Webb, S. (1995) *Poverty Dynamics in Great Britain*. London: Institute for Fiscal Studies.

Weclawowicz, G. (1996) *Contemporary Poland*. London: UCL Press.

Westergaard, J.H. (1978) Social policy and class inequality: some notes on welfare state limits, in R. Miliband and J. Saville (eds) *The Socialist Register 1978*. London: Merlin Press.

Westergaard, J.H. (1995) *Who Gets What?* Cambridge: Polity.

Williams, R. (1962) *The Long Revolution*. London: Chatto & Windus.

Williams, R. (1980) *Problems in Materialism and Culture*. London: Verso.

Williams, R. (1983) *Towards 2000*. London: Chatto & Windus.

Wilson, W.J. (1987) *The Truly Disadvantaged*. Chicago: University of Chicago Press.

Wilson, W.J. (1989) The ghetto underclass: social science perspectives, *Annals of the American Academy of Political and Social Science*, 501: 182–93.

Wilson, W.J. (1992) Another look at 'the truly disadvantaged', *Political Science Quarterly*, 106: 639–56.

Wilson, W.J. and Wacquant, L.D. (1989) The cost of racial and class exclusion in the Inner City, *Annals of the American Academy of Political and Social Science*, 501: 5–25.

Wodz, K. (ed.) (1994a) *Transformation of Old Industrial Regions as a Sociological Problem*. Katowice: Silesian University Press.

Wodz, K. (1994b) The process of marginalization of the traditional workers' communities in Upper Silesia, in K. Wodz (ed.) *Transformation of Old Industrial Regions as a Sociological Problem*. Katowice: Silesian University Press.

Wright, R.E. (1992) A feminization of poverty in Great Britain, *Review of Income and Wealth*, 1: 17–25.

Wright, R.E. (1993) A clarification, *Review of Income and Wealth*, 1: 11–12.

Yérez del Castillo, I. (1994) A comparative approach to social exclusion: Lessons from France and Belgium, *International Labour Review*, 133 (5–6): 613–33.

Index